Freak Weather

Freak Weather

GRAHAM J. McEWAN

ROBERT HALE · LONDON

ISBN 0 7090 4513 1

Robert Hale Limited
Clerkenwell House
Clerkenwell Green
London EC1R 0HT

Photoset in North Wales by
Derek Doyle & Associates, Mold, Clwyd.
Printed in Great Britain by
St Edmundsbury Press, Bury St Edmunds, Suffolk.
Bound by WBC Bookbinders Ltd, Bridgend, Glamorgan.

Contents

Illustrations

FIGURES

PICTURE CREDITS

The following photographs are credited to: Creative Photography: 2, 20. J. Puckett: 3. Philip Micheu: 4. *Liverpool Daily Post and Echo*: 6. *Newham Recorder*: 13. Mrs P.K. Carr: 17. Mrs A.M. Vincent: 18. The *Guardian*: 21, 22.

Figures. *Famous Frosts and Frost Fairs in Great Britain Chronicled from the Earliest to the Present Time* by William Andrews FRHS (Redway, London, 1887): 1, 2, 3. *Frostiana* by G. Davis (G. Davis, London, 1814): 4. *The Everyday Book* by William Hone (Hunt & Clarke, London, 1827): 5. *To the Memory of those who suffered from the Lewes Avalanche in 1836* by W. Thomson (*Sussex Express*, Lewes, 1863): 6. *A Strange Relation of the Suddain and Violent*

Tempest which happened at Oxford, May 31, Anno Domini 1682 by Robert Harrison (Richard Sherlock, Oxford, 1682): 8. *Waterspouts on the Yorkshire Wolds. Cataclysm at Langtoft and Driffield* by J. Dennis Hood (B. Fawcett & Co., Driffield, 1892): 9, 10. *An Account of the Great Floods of August, 1829 in the Province of Moray and Adjoining Districts* by Sir Thomas Dick Lauder (J. McGillivray & Son, Elgin, 1873): 11.

Acknowledgements

My grateful thanks go to the following for providing assistance and information: Mrs Joyce Bennett; S. David Briggs; Mrs P.K. Carr; Mrs Nora Coles; Robert H. Games; Mrs Dorrie Green; Raymond Hyde; A.G. James; Colin Mather; Mrs J. Mitchell; Mrs Elsie Plumb; Mrs Yvonne Roberts; Mrs Sylvia Smith; Miss Judith Tester, and the many people who wrote to me describing their experiences in the east coast floods of 1953, providing a human background to the great disaster.

I should also like to acknowledge my gratitude for the assistance given by the staff of many of our public libraries, and to express special thanks to Theo Brown, FRAI; Chris Hall; Ray Harnett of the National Meteorological Library, and Bob Skinner.

I have attempted to obtain permission for the use of all quotations, but in a few cases I have been unsuccessful in contacting the copyright holders. Any omissions notified to me will be rectified in future editions.

Introduction

It is strange what weather we have had.

Pepys

Man has been aware of the weather since his first conscious thoughts and through a million years has sought to explain it in terms of the wrath or benevolence of gods. In our own time science has taken over from superstition and though today we no longer sacrifice to the deities we are still taken by surprise and are effectively at the mercy of the elements.

From time to time the normal, or average type of weather, becomes extreme, moving outside its usual limits. This book describes examples of weather extremes and their effect on people in the British Isles.

1   The Age of the Frost Fairs

Barring a dramatic change in the British climate, it is highly unlikely that the lower reaches of the Thames will ever freeze over again, yet in past ages this was a fairly frequent occurrence. 'Frost fairs' were sometimes held on the ice. Although early records are possibly inaccurate and almost certainly incomplete, there are records of at least twenty-eight occasions between Roman times and the nineteenth century when the Thames froze over. There are two main reasons why this occurred, the first and obvious one being simply that the winters of the past were colder than they are today, the period between 1650 and 1850 being exceptionally cold and often referred to as 'the little Ice Age'. Frost fairs, occasions of great jollity, were held on the Thames on at least seven occasions during this period, and it has been suggested that our notion of what Christmas weather should be was formed to a large extent by the cold winters of the early nineteenth century. Five of the six winters between 1817 and 1822 were exceptionally cold in the south of England, and in the writings of Charles Dickens, for example, we have on record descriptions of harsh winters and the suffering they caused, offset by Pickwickian scenes of Christmas cheer before the blazing hearth.

The second, less obvious factor, is the changing topography of London and the Thames. The river, like many others in the British Isles in earlier times, was much shallower than it is today, and bordered in many places by extensive marshes, conditions which favoured the formation of ice. The *Anglo-Saxon Chronicle* records that in 1114, following a severe drought, and an exceptionally low tide, it was possible to walk across the Thames river-bed east of London Bridge, and it has been estimated that as late as 1839, the depth of water at the bridge during low spring tides was no more than ten feet. Furthermore, tidal flow in the Thames in past ages was much weaker than in modern times, and this would have encouraged freezing, the tide being slowed still further by the closely packed piers of old London Bridge. Finally there is the tremendous growth in the population of London over the past 150 years, and the consequent continual outpouring into the river of warm water from power-stations, sewers and factories. The temperature of the air itself, possibly for the same reasons, has increased over the centuries, meteorologists G. Manley and T.J. Chandler demonstrating that the air in London today may be some 3°C warmer than it was at the end of the seventeenth century.

The Thames froze at least four times between the first and seventh centuries, but the earliest known occasion on which a frost fair was held seems to be in the year 695, when the river was frozen for six weeks and booths were erected on the ice. It seems likely that such fairs were held during the nine subsequent freezings of the Thames between then and 1564, though historical details are lacking. Such records as do exist, however, indicate how severe the winters of this period were. For example, we know that the Thames was frozen for nine weeks in the year 827; thirteen weeks in 923 and seven weeks in 1061. The ravages of the cold weather destroyed crops, often resulting in famine as in the year 962. In 1035 the chronicler Short records starkly: 'Frost on Midsummer day; all grass and grain and fruit destroyed; a dearth', while in the year 1069 frost and famine were accompanied by plague. The *Harleian Miscellany* states that the earth was frozen hard at the beginning of November, 1076, remaining in this condition until the middle of April the following year, and Cornelius Walford (1827–85) writes that in the winter of 1086, 'The weather was so inclement that in the unusual efforts made to warm houses, nearly all the chief cities of the kingdom were destroyed by fire, including a great part of London and St. Paul's.' Famines followed the winters of 1114/15, 1121/2 and 1209, and the historian Penkethman records that a great frost began at Christmas 1234:

> ...which destroyed the corne in the ground, and the roots and hearbs in the gardens, continuing till Candlemasse [2 February] without any snow, so that no man could plough the ground, and all the yeare after was unseasonable weather, so that barreness of all things ensued, and many poor folks died for the want of victualls.

The winter of 1281/2, according to John Stow (historian and chronicler, 1525–1605), was worse than any man living at that time could remember and 'men passed over the Thames between Westminster and Lambeth dryshod.' Stow also records the freezing of the Thames from below London Bridge to Gravesend in the winter of 1434/5, sea-borne merchandise being landed at the river-mouth and taken over the ice into the heart of London. The

Chronicles of the Grey Friars of London record that the Thames froze in 1410, during 'the most sharpest winter that ever man sawe' and again in 1506, when 'men myght goo with carttes over the Temse and horses, and it lasted tylle Candlemas.'

It is with the coming of the sixteenth century that we learn substantially more about the winters of the past. Raphael Holinshed, for example, records that on New Year's Eve, 1564:

> People went over and alongst the Thames on the ise, from London Bridge to Westminster. Some plaied at the football as boldlie there as if it had been on the drie land; divers of the court being then at Westminster, shot dailie at prickes set upon the Thames; and the people both men and women, went on the Thames in greater numbers than in anie street of the Citie of London.

It is said that Queen Elizabeth ventured on to the ice, though details of her visit are lacking. The thaw came suddenly on the night of 3 January, causing floods all over England, the swollen rivers breaking down bridges, carrying away houses and drowning many people.

According to Francis Drake (historian, 1696–1771), in his *Eboracum: or, the History and Antiquities of York*, an extreme frost commenced at Martinmas (11 November) 1607, the River Ouse being frozen hard enough to bear the weight of carts and carriages. Many sports took place on the ice, including bowling and football, and a horse-race 'was run from the tower at St Mary Gate end along and under the great arch of the bridge to the Crain at Skeldergate postern.'

In 1608 a frost fair was again held on the frozen Thames, an account of which was given by Edmund Howe in his *Continuation of the Abridgement of Stow's English Chronicle* (1611). The frost began on 8 December 1607, and, apart from some intermittent thawing, continued until 2 February the following year. Howe writes that:

> ...all sorts of men, women and children went boldly upon the ice in most parts; some shot at prickes, others bowled and danced, with other variable pastimes; by reason of which concourse of people were many that set up boothes and standings upon the ice, as fruit-sellers, victuallers, that sold beere and wine, shoemakers, and a barber's tent, etc.

In January 1614 there was, according to Drake, 'such a heavy snow upon the earth as was not remembered by any man then living.' The frost commenced on the 26th of that month and continued until 17 March, the thaw causing the River Ouse to surge down North Street and Skeldergate in York and forcing people to leave their houses. Many bridges were washed away, and the inundation, occurring during assize week, caused great disruption to court business. After the thaw the weather was exceptionally hot and dry, and in April the ground was 'as dusty as in any time of summer.'

The severe winters continued: in 1620, according to Edward Walford in his *Old and New London* (1872/3) the frost 'enabled the Londoners to carry on all manner of sports and trades upon the river', and in December 1683 began what is probably the most famous of English winters, later described by R.D. Blackmore in *Lorna Doone*, published in 1869. In *Lorna Doone* he describes the dense fog and bitter wind that preceded the frost; the tameness of hares and birds made desperate by the cold; the freezing of the holy water as it is poured on to the coffin of old Sir Ensor Doone; steaming horses huddled together in their stables with long icicles hanging from their muzzles, and the finding of sheep safe beneath the snow, packed closely together 'as if in a great pie' surrounded by a ribbed cave of yellow snow. Blackmore's memorable description of the great frost includes the following passage:

> That night such a frost ensued as we had never dreamed of, neither read in ancient books, or histories of Frobisher. The kettle by the fire froze, and the crock upon the hearth-cheeks; many men were killed, and cattle rigid in their head ropes. Then I heard that fearful sound, which never I had heard before, neither since have heard (except during that same winter), the sharp yet solemn sound of trees burst open by the frost-blow. Our great walnut lost three branches, and has been dying ever since; though growing meanwhile, as the soul does. And the ancient oak of the cross was rent, and many scores of ash trees. But why should I tell all this? The people who have not seen it (as I have) will only make faces and disbelieve; till such another frost comes; which perhaps may never be.

Blackmore also used the winter of 1814, described later in this chapter, as the background for another work, *Alice Lorraine*, published in 1875.

Another indication of the severity of that same winter is to be found in the parish register of the Holy Rood Church, Southampton, where, among the entries of baptisms for the month of February 1684, is recorded:

1683/4 This yeare was a great Frost, which began before Christmasse, soe that ye 3rd and 4th dayes of this month February ye River of Southampton was frossen all over and covered with ice from Calshott Castle to Redbridge, and Tho: Martaine mar [master] of a vessell went upon ye ice from Berry near Marchwood to Milbrook-point. And ye river at Ichen Ferry was so frossen over that severall persons went from Beauvois-hill to Bittern Farme, forwards and backwards.

Southampton Water in the seventeenth century was much shallower than it is today, and fringed by wide marshes, conditions which encourage the formation of ice, but it was still strongly tidal, and such a thick extensive layer of ice was unprecedented. Nor has it been known since, though parts of the bay froze over in 1879 and in 1895, when Portsmouth Bay was also covered with ice. On neither occasion, however, was the ice strong enough to walk upon.

Another parish register which contains a vivid description of this terrible winter is that of the church of St Bartholomew at Ubley, near Wrington, now in the county of Avon, but formerly in Somerset. It records:

In the year 1683 was a mighty great frost, the like was not seene in England for many ages. It came upon a very deep snow, which fell immediately after Christmas, and it continued untill a Lady-day [25 March]. The ground was not open nor the snow cleane gone off the earth in thirteene weeks. Some of the snow remained at mindipe [Mendips] till midsummer ... people did die so fast that it was the greatest parte of their work (which was appointed to doe that worke) to burie the dead; it being a day's work for two men, or two days work for one man, to make a grave.

The River Thames was frozen from the beginning of December 1683, until early in February the following year, and many broadsheets and pamphlets were printed, commemorating this, perhaps the most famous of London's frost fairs. The diarist John Evelyn, in an entry dated 24 January 1684, described the scene as follows:

The frost continuing more and more severe, the Thames before London, was still planted with boothes in formal streetes, all sorts of trades and shops furnish'd and full of commodities, even to a printing presse, where the people and ladyes tooke a fancy to have their names printed, and the day and yeare set down when printed on the Thames: this humour tooke so universally, that 'twas estimated the printer gain'd £5 a day, for printing a line onely, at sixpence a name, besides what he got by ballads, etc. Coaches plied from Westminster to the Temple, and from several other staires, to and fro, as in the streetes, sleds, sliding with skeetes, a bull-baiting, horse and coach races, puppet-plays, and interludes, cookes, tipling, and other lewd places, so that it seem'd to be a bacchanalian triumph, or carnival on the water.'

Evelyn records that innumerable wild animals and birds died, as well as farm animals and deer in parks. Ports were frozen up, the ships locked in an icy grip, and, there being shortages of food and fuel, money was collected for the benefit of the poor. There was also a considerable water shortage, pipes and pumps being frozen up, this causing not only distress to individuals but also stopping various industries, such as brewing. The streets of London were clogged with the smoke from thousands of coal fires, Evelyn commenting that one could hardly breathe, nor see across the road. Many exotic plants perished, and he comments, like R.D. Blackmore, on trees being split open by the frost. He continues: 'Nor was this severe weather much less intense in most parts of Europe, even as far as Spain in the most southern tracts.'

King Charles II and other members of the royal family descended on to the frozen Thames, and, like the lesser folk, had their names printed, as follows:

CHARLES,	KING
JAMES,	DUKE
KATHERINE,	QUEEN
MARY,	DUTCHESS
ANN,	PRINCESSE
GEORGE,	PRINCE
HANS IN KELDER.	

London: Printed by G. Croom, on the *ICE*, on the River *Thames, January* 31, 1684

Fig.1. The names of the royal family, from a printing-press on the frozen Thames.

'James, Duke' was the Duke of York, the king's brother, later to

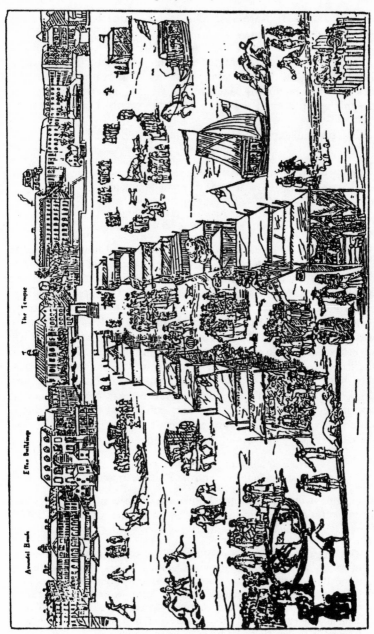

Fig.2. Frost fair on the Thames in 1684

become James II. 'Katherine, Queen' was Catherine de Braganza,
wife of Charles II. 'Mary, Dutchess' was Mary of Modena, second
wife of the Duke of York. 'Ann, Princesse' was the wife of
'George, Prince' (of Denmark) and later to become Queen Anne.
It is thought that the last name on the list is an example of Charles
II's humour, signifying 'Jack in the Cellar', and alluding to the
pregnancy of 'Ann, Princesse': in all, a very distinguished family
party.

G. Croom also printed the following verse on the ice:

> To the print-house go,
> Where Men the art of Printing soon do know,
> Where for a Teaster, you may have your name
> Printed, hereafter for to show the same:
> And sure, in former Ages, ne'er was found
> A Press to print, where men so oft were droun'd!

All manner of amusements are described and illustrated in the
broadsheets: skittles, nine-pins, football, fiddle-playing and
dancing, bull- and bear-baiting. Large boats, some on wheels and
others on runners, decorated with flags and streamers and full of
merrymakers, were pulled hither and thither by watermen
(otherwise out of work because of the ice) and horses. Skating
was, of course, one of the most popular activities and there are
several references to the remarkable agility of some Dutchmen on
the ice – presumably, with their numerous canals and waterways,
they were practised skaters. A tremendous variety of food and
drink was sold on the ice: chicken, turkey, gammon and rabbit;
hot gingerbread and pancakes; tea, coffee and chocolate; beer,
wine and spirits. Near Whitehall an ox was roasted on the ice.
Prices were often exorbitant, one broadsheet recording:

> What you can buy for three pence on the shore,
> Will cost you four pence on the Thames, or more.

The hard winters continued into the eighteenth century, the
Thames freezing over in January 1709 and in the winter of 1715/16;
Dawk's News-Letter of 14 January 1716, reporting:

> The Thames seems now a solid rock of ice; and booths for the sale
> of brandy, wine, ale and other exhilarating liquors, have been for
> some time fixed thereon; but now it is a manner like a town:
> thousands of people cross it, and with wonder view the
> mountainous heaps of water that now lie congealed into ice. On
> Thursday, a great cook's shop was erected, and gentlemen went as
> frequently to dine there, as at any ordinary [shop].

Printing-presses again made their appearance on the ice; coaches, wagons and carts plied to and fro, and an enthusiastic preacher held forth to a motley congregation amongst whom was the Prince of Wales (later George II). It was reported that there was an exceptionally high spring tide on the 14th, this raising the ice and the frost fair *en masse* some fourteen feet, water flooding into low-lying cellars on the river-banks.

Another exceptionally severe winter was that of 1739/40 a frost commencing on Christmas Day which lasted until the 17th February. There were shortages of fuel, food and water, the poor and unemployed suffering greatly, and despite relief funds many people died of the cold. Watermen, fishermen, carpenters, bricklayers and other workmen, carrying their tools, walked through the streets, imploring relief for themselves and their families, a contemporary account recording that, 'to the honour of the British character, this was liberally bestowed'. Enormous damage was caused to shipping in the lower reaches of the Thames a few days after the frost began by a high wind which tore many vessels from their moorings. The ships were smashed against each other, and were ground amongst huge sheets of ice; many carrying much needed corn and coal were sunk, in some cases with their crews. Above London Bridge the Thames was completely frozen over, booths, printing-presses, shops, kitchens, etc., being rapidly erected by traders to take advantage of the novelty of the situation. A group of revellers bought a large ox in Smithfield to be roasted on the frozen river, a man named Hodgeson claiming the privilege of slaughtering the animal, his father having killed the ox roasted on the Thames in the great frost of 1684.

Many other rivers froze, including the Ouse at York: a printer and historian named Thomas Gent related:

It was a dangerous spot on the south side of the bridge, where I first set up, as it were, a kind of press – only a roller wrapped about with blankets. Whilst reading the verses I had made to follow the names – wherein King George was most loyally inserted – some soldiers round about made great acclamation, with other good people; but the ice suddenly cracking, they almost as quickly ran away, whilst I, who did not hear well, neither guessed the meaning, fell to work, and wondered at them as much for retiring so precipitately as they did at me for staying, but, taking courage, they shortly returned back, brought company, and I took some pence amongst them. After this I moved my shop to and fro, to the great satisfaction of young gentlemen and ladies, and others, who were very liberal on the occasion.

When the thaw came several people lost their lives on the Thames as the ice melted, including a well-known fruit-seller, 'Doll the Pippin-woman.' The traders stayed as long as possible, courting disaster to make money while they could. Their precipitous departure was evident on the morning of 21 January, when those living on the west side of London Bridge awoke to find that a motley collection of abandoned booths, tents and huts had floated down on the melting ice to come to rest against the bridge, in an untidy mass of flotsam.

There were several severe winters during the latter half of the eighteenth century, but the Thames does not seem to have frozen sufficiently hard to support another frost fair until the winter of 1788/9 when the *London Chronicle* reported:

> No sooner had the Thames acquired a sufficient consistency than booths, turn-abouts, etc. were erected; the puppet-shows, wild beasts etc. were transported from every adjacent village; while the watermen, that they might draw their usual resources from the water broke the ice close to the shore, and erected bridges with toll-booths, to make every passenger pay a half-penny for getting on to the ice.

The ice at various parts of the river presented different surfaces: in some stretches of a mile or two it was smooth and flat, while in others it was rough and hilly where large quantities of wind-driven snow had accumulated. It was reported that the ice at Blackfriars was eighteen feet thick. On Saturday 10 January, thirteen men arrived at Carlton House with a wagon bearing a ton of coal which they had pulled all the way from Loughborough in Leicestershire to present to the Prince of Wales, later George IV. After the coal was emptied into the cellars, Mr Weltjie, Clerk of the Cellars, gave the men four guineas and when the Prince was informed he gave them a further twenty guineas and ordered a pot of beer for each man. On Tuesday the 13th the Prince donated £1,000 to help the poor and unemployed, of which there were very large numbers. One contemporary account, after describing the scenes of merrymaking on the ice, from Putney Bridge down to Redriff, continues:

> From this description the reader is not, however, to conclude that all was as it seemed. The miserable inhabitants that dwelt in houses on both sides of the river during these thoughtless exhibitions, were many of them experiencing extreme misery; destitute of employment, though industrious, they were with families of helpless children, for want of employment, pining for want of bread

... though liberal subscriptions were raised for their relief, many perished through want and cold.

The frost fair was brought to an abrupt end with the thaw of Tuesday evening, 13 January. At about 8 p.m. the ice began to crack and there were scenes of incredible confusion as 'men, beasts, booths, turn-abouts, puppet-shows etc were all in motion and pouring towards the shore on each side.'

Probably the most severe winter of the following century, during which the last frost fair was held on the Thames, was that of 1813/14. (Fig.3). The great frost was preceded by a thick, widespread fog which descended in the evening of 27 December. As soon as the fog dispersed the snowfalls began, one contemporary account asserting that there 'was nothing in the memory of man to equal these falls.' It was bitterly cold, a freezing wind blowing continually from the north and north-east, and enormous icicles, over three feet long, hung from buildings. Water-pipes froze in houses and stand-pipes were opened in the streets, while the traffic was brought almost to a standstill by the snow. All the ponds and rivers in London were frozen and skating was pursued with great enthusiasm. At the end of January enormous masses of ice floated down the Thames from the upper reaches, and by Sunday the 30th they had blocked the river between Blackfriars and London Bridges. By Tuesday the river was a solid mass of ice, and the watermen placed signs at the ends of all the streets leading to the city side of the river announcing a safe footage across the ice. Thousands of people flocked on to the frozen river where a variety of entertainments had been prepared by the eager entrepreneurs. Among these was the ceremonial roasting of a sheep over a coal fire, sixpence being demanded simply to view the spectacle and a shilling asked and willingly given for a slice of the meat which was termed 'Lapland mutton'.

By the following day, Wednesday 2 February, a grand avenue of booths had been erected between Blackfriars and London Bridges, this being named 'The City Road'. Printing-presses were erected and 'almost every appendage of a fair on land was now transferred to the Thames.' People flocked in ever increasing numbers to the frost fair as, of course did traders and pedlars.

'The greatest rubbish of all sorts', it was reported, 'was raked up and sold at double and treble the original cost. Books and toys labelled "Bought on the Thames" were seen in profusion. The watermen profited exceedingly, for each person paid a toll of two or three pence before he was admitted to Frost Fair; some *douceur*

FROSTIANA:

OR

A HISTORY OF

THE RIVER THAMES

In a Frozen State:

WITH AN ACCOUNT OF

THE LATE SEVERE FROST ;

AND THE WONDERFUL EFFECTS

OF

Frost, Snow, Ice, and Cold,

IN ENGLAND,

AND IN DIFFERENT PARTS OF THE WORLD ;

INTERSPERSED

WITH VARIOUS AMUSING ANECDOTES,

TO WHICH IS ADDED,

THE ART OF SKATING.

A *dreadful winter* came ; *each day* severe,
Misty when mild, and *icy-cold* when clear.
CRABBE.

London :

Printed and published on the ICE on the River *Thames,*
February 5th, 1814, by G. DAVIS.

Sold also by Sherwood, Neely, and Jones, Paternoster Row.

Fig.4. Title page of *Frostiana*.

was also expected on your return. These men are said to have taken six pound in the course of a day.'

Many stayed on the ice until late at night, enjoying the beauty of the moonlit scene.

On the Saturday morning the weather had changed somewhat, with the wind shifting to the south and a light fall of snow. It did not bode well for the frost fair but thousands still went on to the ice, and the merrymaking continued. Some gambled, played at skittles, drank and danced to the music of fiddles, while others sat round large fires, drinking tea and coffee, beer, wine and spirits. Towards the evening, however, rain fell and the ice began to crack. The thaw had begun but still many were reluctant to leave the frozen river. On Saturday night a publican, Mr Lawrence of The Feathers, Queenhithe, left his booth, which was opposite Brook's Wharf, in the care of two men, taking away his liquor but leaving them some gin. At 2 a.m. on the Sunday the tide began to flow and the ice bearing the booth was carried away. By now there were nine men inside, and in their panic they allowed their fire to set the covering of the booth alight. As the blazing booth on its ice floe moved down the river, the nine had to jump for it, and they were lucky to save themselves amidst the confusion by scrambling into a drifting boat also moving downstream with the thawing ice. By three o'clock that afternoon the thaw was well under way with great masses of ice floating down the river, but as late as 2.30 on the Monday afternoon a printing-press was again erected on an island of ice, between Blackfriars and Westminster Bridges, and the title page of a book called *Frostiana* was printed. (Fig.4). At the weekend thousands of people went down to the riverside hoping to visit the frost fair, but they were too late. 'Maybe next year', perhaps they thought, but it was not to be. It was the last of the Thames frost fairs.

2 Ordeals in the Snow

Trapped by Snow

It is possible for human beings to survive for several days beneath a thick, insulating covering of snow. For example, the historian Thomas Hearne (1678–1735), describing the ordeal of a Somerset woman who, in the winter of 1708/9, had lain for seven days beneath snow, wrote:

> She was found to have taken a great part of her upper garment for sustenance; but how she could have digested a textile fabric of wool or flax is not easy to understand. She surprised her neighbours by the assertion that she had lain very warm, and had slept most part of the time. One of her legs lay just under a bush, and was not quite covered with snow; this became in consequence frost-bitten, but not too far for recovery. Her spirits revived, and she was able shortly to resume her ordinary duties.

Many similar cases have been recorded but the most well-documented British case is probably that concerning 42-year-old Elizabeth Woodcock who, in February 1799, spent eight days beneath snow near Impington, a village some five miles to the north-west of Cambridge.

Between six and seven o'clock on the evening of Saturday 2 February, Elizabeth was returning on horseback from Cambridge to Impington. It was a bleak, stormy night with a north-westerly wind and the ground was covered with snow. She was about half a mile from home when her horse was startled by a bright light in the sky, possibly a lightning flash. The horse stepped backwards and Elizabeth, fearing that it would stumble into a nearby ditch, dismounted, intending to lead the animal home. He broke free, however, and galloped off the road and across a field. She ran after him, but her progress was impeded by a basket she was carrying and the loss of one of her shoes, and she chased the animal for about a quarter of a mile before catching it. Taking hold of the bridle she again attempted to lead the horse home, but after

29

retracing her steps to a thicket by the road, she was so fatigued, and her left foot, now lacking a shoe, was so aching with the cold that she could walk no further. She sent the horse off, hoping it would find its way home, and then sat down underneath the trees, the falling snow now beginning rapidly to build up round her. By eight o'clock she was completely covered, the snow above her head soon reaching a thickness of between two and three feet. Numbed by the cold and incapable of movement Elizabeth simply resigned herself to her fate. It may seem strange that she gave in so easily, but other travellers lost in the snow have testified to feeling an overwhelming lethargy, and feelings almost amounting to indifference to their fate. She dozed a little during the night, and in the morning, seeing a hole about six inches across in the snow above her, managed with great difficulty to break off a branch from a nearby bush and thrust it, with her handkerchief attached, through to the surface. Help was not forthcoming though, and Elizabeth spent the next seven days beneath the snow.

She could distinguish perfectly, she later recalled, the alternations of day and night, and was further able to keep track of time by the church bells of neighbouring villages, in particular that of Chesterton, a village about two miles away, where in winter, Elizabeth knew, the church bell was rung at eight o'clock in the evening and four o'clock in the morning. She could also hear carriages on the road, the bleating of sheep and the barking of dogs. On one occasion she heard two gypsies talking – they were discussing a donkey they had lost – and shouted as loudly as she could, but the snow muffled her voice and they did not hear.

At the end of the week a thaw set in and the snow around Elizabeth began to melt, the cavity in which she was entombed enlarging to about three-and-a-half feet high by about two feet wide. The hole above her became greatly enlarged and she thought of trying to escape, but was too weak and faint, all feeling having gone from her arms and legs. Her clothes were soaked through and for the first time she began to despair of being found, but rescue was at hand.

At about 12.30 p.m. on Sunday 10 February, Joseph Muncey, a young farmer, passed close to where Elizabeth was buried and saw her handkerchief on the stick. Walking closer to the hole in the snow, he heard the sound of Elizabeth's laboured breathing. He immediately called to another farmer and a shepherd who were nearby, and the latter, John Stittle, shouted through to Elizabeth. She replied very faintly, imploring them to help her out of the snow and Stittle cleared some of the snow away, reaching through to grasp her hand. Her husband was sent for and soon arrived with some neighbours, a horse and cart and blankets. The snow was further cleared away and a biscuit and some brandy were passed through to her, but as she was moved she fainted, and her rescuers waited until she came round before placing her gently in the cart, covering her with blankets and driving her home.

Elizabeth's horse had arrived home on the night she was trapped in the snow and her husband had set out with a lantern to try to find her. With neighbours he continued searching over the next few days. It was thought at one point that she might have been robbed and murdered by gypsies and several of their huts were searched; and with fading hopes, they were still seeking her when she was so unexpectedly discovered.

Fig.5. Elizabeth Woodcock, an illustration from Hone's *Everyday Book*, vol.2.

Elizabeth was put to bed and fed on broth until something of her strength returned, but sadly she never fully recovered from her ordeal and died five months later.

The Lewes Avalanche

White Christmasses are comparatively rare in England, the *Guinness Book of Records* stating that London has experienced snow at Christmas on only seven occasions since 1900. They were more frequent during the nineteenth century, a notable example being the Christmas of 1836 when, at the unlikely location of Lewes in Sussex, occurred the most disastrous avalanche ever recorded in the United Kingdom.

The weather prior to Christmas had been mild and damp, but on Saturday, Christmas Eve, the wind veered round from the south-west to the north-east, and brought with it a heavy fall of snow, which continued, almost without a break, until Monday. The whole country was affected, but the mid-Sussex coastal strip was exceptionally hard hit, with Brighton and Lewes almost completely cut off. The snow had been driven by gale force winds into drifts of up to twenty feet and in Brighton hundreds of people had to dig their way out of their homes.

On Christmas Eve, a Mr Thompson of Lewes was returning home from London. The coach left at 2 p.m. and made good time until it arrived at East Grinstead, when the snow began to fall very heavily. By the time the coach reached Ashdown Forest the road was obliterated, and the horses struggled through snow-drifts before they reached Lewes, two hours late. Mr Thompson continues his story:

> The following day was Sunday and Christmas Day, and the non-arrival of letters plainly informed us that the roads had become impassable, and although but little snow fell after this day, yet so great had been the fall, that for nearly a week all intercourse with London was cut off.

The prolonged winds had the bizarre effect of depositing an enormous ridge of snow on the sloping top of an almost perpendicular chalk cliff, 300 feet high, above a group of cottages called Boulder Row in South Street at the Cliffe end of Lewes. The drift was between ten and fifteen feet thick and blown by the wind into fantastic shapes resembling ocean waves; it hung menacingly directly above the cottages, but seems to have been regarded by the inhabitants more as a curiosity than a danger, even when one old man said he remembered that, about fifty years earlier, a similar drift had come crashing down with tremendous violence, demolishing houses and carrying everything before it into the River Ouse. Further warning came on the evening of 26 December when part of the drift fell, demolishing a sawing-shed in a neighbouring timber-yard owned by Charles Wille. Mr Wille immediately went to warn the cottagers, as did Robert Hyams who owned the Schooner beer shop, nearly opposite Boulder Row, and a few wisely moved out, but most insisted on staying.

Next morning the danger was even more evident, several large fissures being observed in the mass of snow, and the inhabitants of Boulder Row were again warned, the *Sussex Weekly Advertiser* commenting: 'Some of them upon this came out, but others (although places of refuge were offered them) persisted, by some fatal infatuation, remaining and endeavouring to remove their effects.' At about 10.15 a.m. Robert Hyams, realizing that an avalanche was imminent, rushed, with a Mr. T. Morris, into the passageway at the rear of Boulder Row, pleading with the inhabitants to leave. Incredibly, they still refused to go, and Hyams even tried unsuccessfully to drag two women out by force, before himself fleeing. A few moments later an enormous mass of snow slid off the cliff and crashed on to Boulder Row. An eyewitness described how the avalanche seemed to heave the end seven cottages upwards and then break over them like a gigantic wave, carrying them almost across the road which was about thirty-five feet wide. When the mist of powdered snow had settled there was nothing to be seen but a vast white mound. According to the *Sussex Weekly Advertiser*:

> The scene which followed was heart-rending. Children were screaming for their parents, and women were rushing through the streets with frantic gestures in search of their offspring; while in the midst of this consternation men were hastening from all quarters with spades and shovels for the purpose of extricating the sufferers. In an incredibly short space of time a large number of labourers was at work in the most orderly and effective manner in removing the mass under the superintendence of the petty constables of the Cliffe, and several influential persons who aided the exertions of the men by their own personal example and encouragement.

Among the 'influential persons' was Mr Thompson who had left his home at about 9.30 that morning with the intention of walking to the top of the Middle Downs, to view the Sussex Weald with its covering of snow. He was met on the way, however, by John Hoper, a solicitor from Lewes, who ran towards him, shouting that

a great fall of snow had killed many people, and begging for help.
Mr Hoper was afraid to return to the scene, but Mr Thompson was
made of sterner stuff, apparently being one of those characters
who come into their own during a crisis. He reported:

> I waited not for further particulars but at once hastened to the spot
> where I conjectured the mischief must be, not many minutes
> elapsed ere I reached the place, and found of course great
> confusion. My first endeavour was to obtain something like order,
> therefore I sent for the Constable of the Cliffe, Mr Britton, a
> gentleman conducting a large school there, who kindly came
> immediately and forming a ring, kept back the anxious and
> increasing crowd from impeding the necessary labours.

The long job of removing the debris was begun, one group of men
shovelling the snow from the cottages while others then threw it
into the nearby River Ouse. In a short time a boy, Jeremiah
Rooke, was unearthed alive, but badly bruised and with a
fractured thigh. The rescuers then found the body of a Mrs Taylor,
who had left her cottage early that morning, fearing the very
disaster that had occurred. She had returned to fetch a shawl for
her baby and was then caught in the fall, being swept across the
road to the wall opposite. Her body, however, had shielded the
child, and miraculously the little one was dug out alive. Now
bodies were being uncovered: Joseph Wood, fifteen; Mary Bridgeman, eleven; her mother, Maria Bridgeman; and another house-
wife, Phoebe Barnden.

As the rescue team approached the upper storey of a house
belonging to one Henry Boaks, they heard a voice crying out from
beneath the snow. It was his mother-in-law, Mrs Sherlock, who
was discovered lying face downwards on the floor, a bedstead
shielding her and two babies she was clutching. When it was
realized that all three were alive, a cheer arose from the rescue
party. Sadly, however, Jane Boaks, the mother of the two
children, had been killed, her body being found nearby. Also
uncovered was the body of William Geer, an elderly man who had
occupied the first floor of one of the cottages.

The backbreaking work had now continued for most of the day,
Mr Thompson recording that he 'cheered the men at their work
and ordered them to be liberally supplied with beer.' Stretchers
and blankets were obtained, the dead and injured being taken to
the nearby workhouse where several doctors were working hard.
There was still a large mass of snow on the brow of the hill, where
the resourceful Mr Thompson, realizing that it might fall at any

moment, dispatched a team of workmen, under the supervision of a local architect, to cut through it. He reported:

> In order that the force of any falling mass should be broken, the work at the covered houses was reversed, and by casting the snow towards the hill an embankment was raised, which might intercept any falling portion from the workmen below ... I promised the workmen that I would fix my attention on the snow above, and give timely notice of any falling quantity. A signal from the brow of the hill (which as I have before stated was at least 300 feet high) gave me intimation, and as I exclaimed Run! the workmen started for their lives, and a second mass came thundering down.

Mr Thompson was partially covered by the snow, and one of the rescue party, Mr Phillips, a builder, was buried up to his neck; luckily though, no one was hurt and the work continued. Just before this second fall, moaning had been heard coming from beneath the snow and another member of the Bridgeman family, John, a lad of fifteen, was found. He was covered with debris, lying in the passageway which ran along the back of the cottages. He was still alive after six hours beneath the snow, and the rescuers had cleared his arm and hand when the second avalanche occurred. He survived this, but the rescue team experienced great difficulty in extricating him, wedged as he was by timber and masonry. A rafter pinning his fractured leg was sawn through, a nerve-racking operation as it seemed only too likely that the removal of the rafter might cause a heavier piece of timber to fall and crush the boy's chest. While they were working to free him, John pleaded for a drink and was given a few mouthfuls of beer, and later some brandy and water. He was finally removed safely and taken to the workhouse for treatment. He told rescuers that Susan Hayward, the only remaining inhabitant of the cottages still unaccounted for, was buried in the same passageway and, shortly after, her lifeless body was discovered there. The rescue work was over, Mr Thompson concluding his day's efforts by placing a guard over the ruins before returning home.

Of the fifteen people buried by the avalanche, eight had been killed, a further five had broken limbs or severe bruising and two, very young children, were uninjured. Had the avalanche occurred a few hours earlier the death toll would almost certainly have been much higher, for some forty people had been sleeping in the cottages the night before the disaster. Many of these, however, had gone out early to view the arctic landscape in the brilliant sunshine.

The following day a further inspection was made of the ruins. It was a tragic spectacle, with domestic possessions – clothes, furniture, pots, pans and broken pottery – exposed to public gaze and hopelessly jumbled together with snow and debris. The wreckage was littered with pathetic reminders of Christmas – scraps of holly and mistletoe, pieces of cake and plum pudding. Parties of men went up on the cliff again and cut out trenches through the remaining snow to prevent a further massive fall and although that evening another snowfall wrecked a house in which corn was stored, there were no further casualties.

One of the survivors, Mrs Sherlock, later described her ordeal:

> My daughter-in-law and I were sitting by the fire at about a quarter past ten dressing and washing the children, when Mrs Potter came in and told us to be quick and dress the baby for we must go – they expected the snow to fall on the houses every moment. She had been gone about a minute or two when it came over at once pitch dark. We were all flung down. I fell close to the bed, and I could feel part of the bedstead come over me. My daughter-in-law, I think, fell with her head against the chest of drawers. She moaned very much. After some time the baby moved and cried. I pushed it on to her, and said, 'Jane, try and give the baby the breast.' She said 'I've done that for the last time, mother.' After that, I heard the noise of people overhead; I slipped my hand along and took hold of hers, and told her to keep her spirits up for I heard the noise of spades above, and I was sure they would dig us out. She made no answer, but only screamed, then she was dead. I then laid as still as I could till we were dug out.

On the evening of 27 December a meeting was held at the Bear Inn to make arrangements for a public appeal. £394.5s.6d. was raised, £126.5s.6d. covering the labour and expenses incurred in the rescue work, and £193 being given to the families to replace the clothes and furniture they had lost. The remaining £75 was placed in a bank account for the benefit of eight children orphaned or injured by the avalanche, the fund to be administered by the incumbent vicar of the parish 'for the purposes of their advancement in life'.

The inquest was held on the morning of Wednesday 28 December 1836, the jury viewing the eight bodies in the workhouse. They returned a verdict of accidental death, praising the prompt and efficient services of the medical men of Lewes.

With the exception of Susan Hayward, all those killed in the Lewes avalanche were buried in a mass grave in South Malling churchyard. The roads were still blocked by snow, a deep cutting

---

This Tablet

Is placed here by Subscription, to Record an
Awful Instance of

THE UNCERTAINTY OF HUMAN LIFE.

On the Morning of.Dec. 27, 1836,

The Poorhouses of this Parish was destroyed by a

MASS OF SNOW

FALLING FROM THE HILL ABOVE,

And the following Eight individuals were buried beneath
the ruins :—

	Aged		Aged
William Geer	82	M. A. Bridgeman	28
Phœbe Barnden	45	Jane Boaks	25
Mary Taylor	42	Joseph Wood	15
Susan Hayward	34	Mary Bridgeman	11

Their remains are interred on the North side of this
Church.

" Be ye therefore ready also, for the Son of Man cometh at an
hour when ye think not."—*Luke* xii. 40.

Fig.6. Tablet commemorating the victims of the Lewes Avalanche in 1836

being made to allow the passage of the wagons bearing the coffins, and despite the freezing weather a large crowd assembled to watch the interment. A marble tablet was placed in the church recording the 'uncertainty of human life'. (Fig.6)

The disaster is also commemorated in the name of a public house, The Snowdrop.

A Night on the Long Mynd

One of the oddest exhibits in Rowley's House Museum in Shrewsbury is a pair of old boots in a glass case. These boots were worn by the Reverend E. Donald Carr during his incredible ordeal on the Long Mynd on the bitterly cold night of Sunday 29 January 1865.

The Long Mynd (now owned by the National Trust) is a hill of

ancient grits and shales about ten miles long and four miles wide,
its highest part being 1,695 feet above sea level. The slopes on the
northern side, looking towards Shrewsbury, are fairly gentle, but
the face of the south-eastern, or Church Stretton, edge is rocky and
precipitous with deep ravines through which run many small
streams.

The flat summit of the Long Mynd is covered with gorse and
heather and at one time the poorer inhabitants of the area flocked
there to pick and sell the bilberries which grow there in great
profusion. The Reverend Mr Carr wrote that he knew of no more
picturesque sight than the Long Mynd on an August afternoon,
with kettles steaming on fires amongst the heather, and chattering
groups of women and children clustered round, resting after a hard
day's bilberry-picking. In winter, however, it was a different story
and several people perished while attempting to cross the Long
Mynd on dark, cold nights. There were localities with names such
as 'Dead Man's Hollow' and 'Dead Man's Beach' and the last fair
held at Church Stretton before Christmas was known as 'Dead
Man's Fair' after several men lost their lives when making their
way home from the fair across the hills, on a treacherous
November night.

The Reverend Mr Carr had become the Rector of Woolstaston
in 1855 and also ministered to the people in the parish of
Ratlinghope which nestled in a narrow valley at the foot of the
western slope of the Long Mynd; Ratlinghope had for some time
been without a Sunday service and Mr Carr had altered his second
service at Woolstaston from 3 p.m. to 6 p.m. to allow him to take
an afternoon service at Ratlinghope.

The only direct route between Woolstaston and Ratlinghope
was by footpaths over the highest part of the Long Mynd, in
distance about four miles. It was a pleasant journey in summer but
difficult and dangerous in winter when the tracks were covered
with ice, or when fog blanketed the hills or thick snow obscured
every landmark. Whenever possible Mr Carr rode on horseback
between the two churches, but often he was forced to make the
journey on foot. In the eight-and-a-half years of his incumbency he
made the trip almost 2,500 times, priding himself on the fact that
he had not left the church of Ratlinghope once without a Sunday
service. He came to have an intimate knowledge of the geography
of the Long Mynd, feeling quite at home there in all weathers, and
had even crossed it late one November night in thick fog without
mishap.

The week before Mr Carr's ordeal had seen exceptionally heavy snowfalls, strong winds blowing the snow into deep drifts; it was in fact the worst winter since 1814, more than fifty years earlier. Communication between neighbouring villages almost ceased, the Rector commenting that 'letters wont to be received in the morning arrived late in the day or not at all.' The morning service at Woolstaston on 29 January was very poorly attended and Mr Carr thought it unlikely that he would even be expected at Ratlinghope. However, he thought it his duty at least to attempt the journey. He set out on horseback, with a servant, immediately after the morning service, stopping only to swallow some soup and put a flask of brandy in his pocket. He knew only part of the journey would be possible for the horses, but in only half a mile the snow became too deep and he sent them home with the servant. He struggled on through the snow, crossing the deepest drifts on his hands and knees. The open moorland stretched all around him, an unbroken expanse of white, which in the bright sunshine dazzled the rector's eyes, but the general contours of the land were still recognizable and he floundered through the drifts till finally reaching Ratlinghope at 3.15 p.m., two and a quarter hours after leaving Woolstaston. No one had really expected him, but a small congregation had gathered, and Mr Carr conducted a short service before setting out on his homeward journey. The weather, however, had now become menacing, as the rector later described:

> A furious gale had come on from ESE, which as soon as I got on the open moorland, I found was driving clouds of snow and icy sleet before it. It was with considerable difficulty that I made my way up the western ascent of the hill, as I had to walk in the teeth of this gale. The force of this wind was most extraordinary. I have been in many furious gales, but never in anything to compare with that, as it took me off my legs, and blew me flat down upon the ground over and over again.

The sleet stung the rector's face and eyes, making it almost impossible for him to lift his head, and visibility in the blizzard was a few yards. Mr Carr, however, knew exactly where he was, having just passed the half-buried skeleton of a mountain pony which he had noticed on his outward journey, and soon reached another landmark, a pool in a hollow between the hills which was well known to naturalists as the resort of curlews and other birds. From here his route would lead him to a plantation of fir trees, and the remaining part of the journey under their shelter should be comparatively easy. It was at this point, however, that his luck ran out. The blizzard had increased in fury, visibility being almost nil, and he was forced to crawl much of the way up the hill. He struggled on, hoping to see the plantation, but was blown over several times and lost his bearings. He soon realized that he had wandered off course, but was not very worried, thinking that he had gone a little to the south of the plantation and that if he continued further he would soon reach an inhabited district known as Bullock's Moor. He continues:

> Under this impression I walked cheerfully on, but only for a few steps further. Suddenly my feet flew from under me, and I found myself shooting at a fearful pace down the side of one of the steep ravines which I had imagined lay far away to my right. I thought to check myself by putting my stick behind me, and bearing heavily upon it in the manner usual in Alpine travelling. Before, however, I could do so I came in contact with something which jerked it out of my hand and turned me round, so that I continued my tremendous glissade head downwards, lying on my back.'

The rector was convinced that he would be dashed over the rocks at the bottom of the ravine but with a supreme effort he managed to stop his headlong descent. Now, though, not knowing into which ravine he had fallen, he realized that he was lost and that it was unlikely he could live through the night.

He was determined though to make every effort to survive, and knew that his only chance was to keep moving, so he began to make his way laboriously up the opposite side of the ravine, but with no idea as to the direction he was taking. He was puzzled by what looked like a small shadow flitting about on the snow, and putting down his hand was astonished to find that he had touched the head of a hare. He was to see many of these in the course of the night, gambolling and frisking or sitting in holes in the snow, 'well protected by their warm coats, happier far than their human fellow-sufferer who knew that for him there must be no rest that night if he would see the light of another day.' The rector reached the crest of the hill and battled his way along it for some distance before losing his footing and again falling into a ravine. It was a more terrifying experience than his earlier fall – he was thrown one way then the other, sometimes head first, sometimes feet first, sometimes sideways, till at last he managed to halt his flight by clutching at some gorse bushes and digging his feet into the snow. Mr Carr was by now in a pitiable condition; in this second fall he had lost his hat and his warm fur gloves, which he had been wearing over an older pair of dogskin gloves, and his hands

A typical funnel cloud.

Note the lengthening spinning air column

A giant tree comes to rest on a bungalow at Upton, Wirral, in the hurricane of 1990

The massive Selborne Yew, brought down by the hurricane
of 1990

A load of hay was deposited in a garden at St Asaph, north
Wales, when a passing lorry was blown over in the gales of 1990

Waves batter historic Fort Perch Rock at New Brighton, flooding
the promenade and smashing railings during the 1990 hurricane

Another view of Fort Perch Rock in the Mersey estuary,
pounded by mountainous waves in the hurricane of 1990

became so numb that they were nearly useless. A great mass had formed on his whiskers, which soon became a long crystalline beard hanging half-way to his waist, his hair was frozen into a solid block and he had frequently to break away ice which formed round his eyes and below his knees. The rector attempted to tie his handkerchief over his head but his frozen fingers were incapable of forming a knot, and he could only keep it in position by holding it in his teeth. Nor could he refasten his overcoat, which had become unbuttoned in his second fall. Totally exhausted and weak from lack of food, falling at every few steps, he experienced an overwhelming desire to give up his struggle and lie down in the snow, but knew that if he did so he 'would never wake up in this life.'

The rector longed desperately for dawn knowing that a glimpse of the landscape would enable him to fix his location. The wind had now dropped and the stillness was so oppressive that he often spoke aloud for the sake of hearing his own voice, and to reassure himself that the intense cold had not deprived him of the power of speech. The only signs of life were the hares, still sporting on the hillsides.

Dawn eventually came but Mr Carr's ordeal was still not over, for a dense fog enveloped the hills, obscuring everything but the nearest objects. He was now suffering from snow blindness, as he realized when he tried to look at his watch which 'resembled an orange seen through a mist'. He also experienced illusions; gorse bushes in the snow appeared like trees and enclosures, and rocks covered with heather resembled dead animals.

As the day grew brighter he saw that he was walking along the side of an extremely deep ravine, so steep that he could go neither up nor down, causing him to clutch at tufts of vegetation to keep his footing and he progressed for an hour in this manner before the side of the ravine became less steep, and, following the sound of running water, he reached the stream at the bottom of the valley. Though he did not know it at the time, it led to the first cascade of the Light Spout waterfall. The rector continues:

> Hearing the noise of falling water, and seeing dimly rocks around me, I found it would not do to go forward in this direction, so having unconsciously gone to the very edge of the lower cascade, where I must in all probability have been killed had I fallen over, I turned sharply up the hill again, going over the rocks above, and coming down again by a very steep place. Round and round this waterfall I seemed to have climbed in every possible direction.

The rector gave up his attempt to follow the stream and decided to climb to higher ground. Struggling through a deep snow-drift he lost one of his boots and, soon after, the second one. In fact, losing the boots caused Mr Carr no great discomfort for his feet were absolutely numb with cold, and he walked over gorse bushes without feeling the slightest pain.

For many hours he scrambled on, but as he finally felt his endurance waning, heard, to his incredulous delight, the sound of children's voices talking and laughing. The sounds confirmed the rector's belief that he had been walking in the direction of Carding Mill Valley. To his bitter disappointment, however, his shouts for help were followed by total silence and it transpired that the children, playing in the snow, had been terrified at the sudden appearance of Mr Carr, who must indeed have presented an amazing sight with his ice-encrusted head and beard of icicles. He stumbled on, following the direction from which the children's voices had come, and realized that he was now very close to the carding-mill. A little girl ran back to him and he explained that he was the clergyman of Ratlinghope and that he had been lost in the snow all night. She stared at him for a few moments and then said, 'Why, you look like Mr Carr of Woolstaston.' 'I am Mr Carr', replied the rector, and several boys now ran up and helped him to walk to the cottages by the carding-mill. For the moment he was simply overjoyed to find himself back among his fellow human beings and saved from a lonely and miserable death on the Long Mynd.

Incredibly, after resting for only about a quarter of an hour and having been supplied with food, tea, a hat, dry socks and boots, Mr Carr set out again on foot, accompanied by a cottager from the carding-mill, his one thought being to reach his home. Arriving at Church Stretton at about two o'clock, he sent his companion to fetch a doctor and made his own way to the Crown Inn where his adventure aroused great astonishment. With the exception of his fifteen-minute rest at Carding Mill he had been walking without interruption for twenty-two hours! He was given some of the landlord's clothes, these being far too large for him, he wrote, giving a very comical effect. The doctor arrived, dressed the rector's middle finger which had been badly cut and partially skinned; and apart from this all that was needed was hot brandy and water. A fly was ordered to take Mr Carr home, with a second horse for him to ride on the last two miles of his journey where a wheeled vehicle would be unable to get through the snow.

But still he was not home, and on the last, agonizingly slow, stage of his journey on foot through snow-blocked lanes, impassable even for the horse, Mr Carr encountered a messenger from the rectory bearing letters reporting that he was now given up for dead. Mr Carr wrote:

> I sent this messenger back again pretty quickly, and told him to go back as fast as he could and say I was coming. This news reached the village about half an hour before I could get up there myself, and as may be supposed there was great rejoicing. So completely had all hope of my safety been given up, that to my people it seemed almost like a resurrection from the dead.

Rescue parties had made the greatest efforts to find Mr Carr, and though a body was found it was that of a Mr Easthope. This poor man had either sat down to rest or had fallen and rapidly lost consciousness in the intense cold.

The rector's friends said later that they would scarcely have recognized him, dressed as he was in another man's clothes, haggard and shrunken with terribly bloodshot eyes. He was put to bed at once and his hands and feet were rubbed with snow to prevent frostbite; over the following weeks hundreds of gorse prickles worked their way out of his hands and feet.

On 10 February, after the rector's recovery, a special thanksgiving service was held at Woolstaston Church, followed by a celebratory dinner at the rectory attended by the thirty members of the search parties.

Mr Carr's boots were later recovered by parishioners, who retraced his journey over the Long Mynd. They now stand, after a century and more, in Rowley's House Museum, a strange testimony to a story of astonishing endurance.

3 Deluges

Put very simply, the process of rainfall depends on the natural law that warm air holds more water vapour than cold air. When moist warm air rises it becomes cooler, and the moisture is released as rain. Once the rain has fallen, it lies in temporary storage on the ground in rivers, lakes and seas until evaporated again into the air. The collective name for showers of rain, hail, sleet and snow is precipitation, and by the early nineteenth century this was recognized as part of the perpetual recycling of the earth's fixed supply of water. However, the problem of how cloud droplets suspended in air managed to gain sufficient size to fall to the ground remained, and even today the exact mechanics of raindrop formation are the subject of some debate.

As early as the seventeenth century Richard Townley, from the village of Townley near Burnley in Lancashire, was systematically measuring rainfall, keeping a continuous record between 1677 and 1703, but the first person to realize the importance of a national rainfall review was probably George James Symons (1838–1900). His interest in the weather began with the drought years of 1854–58 and he started collecting rainfall statistics from observers in England and Wales, gradually extending his coverage over the British Isles until, at the time of his death in 1900, some 1,500 observers, known collectively as the British Rainfall Organization, were contributing to his annual publication *British Rainfall*. The organization was taken over by the Meteorological Office in 1919, and observers now total over 7,000, of whom about a third are private individuals.

Rain is measured in linear units and gives a depth of rain which would cover absolutely flat, impermeable ground in a specified period. Such ideal surfaces do not occur naturally, so sample rainfalls are gathered from many rain gauges and an average calculated. The simplest type of rain gauge consists of a funnel five or eight inches in diameter which collects the rain and pours it into a container. Every morning at nine o'clock GMT the water is emptied into a graduated glass and the amount recorded. This type of gauge is often used in conjunction with other instruments such as the recording gauge which charts rainfall on a graph. The smallest amount measured is 0.1 mm, or 1/250 of an inch; if the rain is less the word 'trace' is entered in the register.

On average, London experiences twenty-four inches of rain a year, a total which helps us to appreciate the figures on the chart below listing exceptionally rainy days in England. Holding the record is Martinstown, Dorset, where, during a deluge on 18 May 1955, eleven inches of rain fell in a fifteen-hour period. However, there have been deluges of even greater intensity. They are often referred to as cloudbursts, but point precipitation is a more correct term. During such episodes phenomenal quantities of rain, far in excess of the figures below, descend on very small areas, often leaving the surrounding territory totally dry. Indeed, they are frequently so localized as to be missed completely by the rain gauges, leaving the experts to estimate the quantities of rain which have fallen.

The intensity of such falls, however, is all too evident for they may cause severe floods, and witnesses have described the strange phenomenon of great columns of water pouring from the clouds.

Date	Location	Period	Inches
12 July 1900	Ilkley, Yorks.	1¼ hrs	3.75
26 Aug. 1912	Norwich	14 hrs	6.6
29 May 1920	Louth, Lincs.	3 hrs	4.7
16 May 1924	Cannington, Som.	4½ hrs	8.5
16 July 1947	Wisley, Surrey	1¼ hrs	4.0
15 May 1952	Longstone Barrow, Exmoor	12 hrs	8.9
18 July 1955	Martinstown, Dorset	15 hrs	11.0
11 June 1956	Hewenden Reservoir, Yorks.	2 hrs	6.1
7 Oct. 1960	Horncastle, Lincs.	5 hrs	7.2
5 July 1963	Hemyock, Devon	1¼ hrs	3.1
14 Aug. 1975	Hampstead, London	2½ hrs	6.7
13 June 1979	Embsay Moor, Yorks.	53 mins	2.1
9 July 1981	Littleover, Derby.	70 mins	3.1
5 Aug. 1981	Manchester Airport	1 hr	1.7
6 Aug. 1981	Crouch End, G. London	1 hr	2.8

Fig. 7. Some notable British rainfalls

Probably the earliest known example of this phenomenon is that described by Robert Harrison in a booklet entitled *A Strange Relation of the Suddain and Violent Tempest which happened at Oxford May 31 Anno Domini 1682*. (see Fig.8).

A
Strange Relation

Of the Suddain and Violent

TEMPEST,

VVhich happened at *Oxford* May 31.
Anno Domini 1 6 8 2.

Together
With an Enquiry into the probable Caufe
and ufual confequients of fuch like
Tempeſts and *Storms.*

Printed for *Richard Sherlock* Bookfellour in *Oxford,*
ANNO. DOM. 1682.

Fig. 8. Title page of Robert Harrison's booklet

The storm broke early in the afternoon, with lightning, thunder, strong winds and intense darkness. Robert Harrison writes:

> The rain was thick, strong, and ponderous ... several of the drops were extended to the full breadth of a six-penny piece, which also followed one another so closely that they seemed one continuous spout or stream; so that in less than half of a quarter of an hour, these pouring cataracts raised the water in a round and uniform vessel of about 4 foot diameter, near two foot higher than before.'

E.L. Hawke, writing in *Nature* of February 1952, estimated that this information suggests a rainfall figure of about three inches per minute. Compare this with the rainfall figures in Fig.7.

Another account came from Dr. D.P. Thomson who described in the *Philosophical Magazine* a 'waterspout' which burst on Bredon Hill in Gloucester on 3 May 1849. At about 5.30 that afternoon, during a storm of thunder, lightning and hail, an enormous body of water was seen to rush down a gully in Bredon Hill and then alter its course towards the village of Kemerton. The stream was broad and powerful and on reaching the residence of the Reverend W.H. Bellairs, writes Dr Thomson:

> ...broke down a stone wall which surrounded the garden, burst through the foundation of another, made a way for itself through the dwelling house, and then carried off a third wall of brick six feet high. The garden soil was washed away, and enormous blocks of stone and debris from the hill left in its place. By this time the current was considerably broken, nevertheless it flowed through the house to the depth of nearly three feet, for the space of an hour and forty minutes. The neighbouring railway was so deeply flooded as to delay the express train, by extinguishing the fire of the engine.

The following Saturday morning Mr Bellairs traced the course of the torrent, twenty to thirty feet wide, and more than a mile in length, on Bredon Hill. The water had smashed down every wall in its path and removed most, if not all, of the soil. At the north-west shoulder of the hill he found the place where the deluge had commenced, a barley field of about five acres, most of the crop having been beaten down flat and hard as if an enormous body of water had suddenly dropped upon it. Beyond and around this field there was little if any evidence of the deluge. The Reverend W.H. Bellairs comments:

> The general depth of the torrent was from six to seven feet, though in one instance marks upon a tree were met with sixteen feet above the ground. We must not overlook, however, the bending of the

tree under the power of the stream; consequently, though the mark would lead to the belief that the water had risen sixteen feet, it does not follow that it actually did so.

We have another account of a deluge in 1878: at about five o'clock on the evening of Thursday 14 June, Mr E. Wethered from the village of Weston, which lies between Kelston Hill and Bath, was travelling home on a Midland Railway train bound for Weston Station. Looking towards Kelston Round Hill he was struck by the blackness and lowness of the clouds in the vicinity, and suddenly there was a flash of lightning followed by an exceptionally heavy fall of rain. Arriving in Weston Mr Wethered found a great commotion, and was told that, shortly after five o'clock, a tremendous volume of water had advanced like a tidal wave along the Kelston Road, flooding houses, submerging the main road to a depth of four feet and carrying a boulder weighing a quarter of a ton for several yards. Mr Wethered immediately linked the flood with the cloud he had just seen, and made his way towards Kelston Hill where it was obvious that something extraordinary had occurred:

Near the end of the lane (Northbrook) leading to some fields, the hedge on the right for some yards was lying in the road, but the field beyond at this point presented only the appearance of an ordinary storm, while the lane itself was like the bed of a river. To the left was a field of standing grass; for about twelve feet from the hedge the grass remained intact, then for about the same distance it was as though it had been mown down. This torrent, for such it might have been compared to, came to almost a sudden termination a little above the end of the lane, but it extended down the hill till it was joined by two others, one of which had carried a hedge away bodily.

The increased volume of water then poured down over some gardens, uprooting trees and vegetables, in less than ten minutes the hedges were lost sight of, and the water rose to a height of eight feet. This was occasioned by a blockage caused by an arch, which carried off the water from a small stream, not being large enough to take the increased volume. Finally it burst over, scooping the ground out in front of some cottages several feet deep and flowed on as a river some yards wide, again destroying gardens in which were valuable stocks of vegetables.

There had been five distinct torrents altogether, these uniting to rush in a body on the village of Weston before draining off into the River Avon. Other witnesses in the vicinity of Kelston Hill reported that, after a still, sultry day, clouds had gathered over the hill at about 4.30 p.m. and at 5.30 there was a tremendous clap of thunder followed by a terrific downpour 'in bucketfulls', as it was described. Most of the water fell under the brow of the hill where '*it came down in several columns*' (my italics). The storm which was accompanied by a heavy fall of hail covering the ground to a depth of several inches was estimated to have caused at least £2,000 worth of damage.

More serious than the incidents so far described was the disaster which occurred at Swansea on Saturday morning, 3 September 1886, when a severe thunderstorm passed over South Wales and the Midlands. By noon the weather had brightened somewhat but, at about three o'clock, the skies began to darken again, as the thunder returned, accompanied by tremendous torrents of rain which continued uninterrupted for some twenty minutes. At both Swansea and the Mumbles, vast rivers of rainwater rushed down the hillsides, making deep courses in the centre of the roads, but the worst destruction occurred in the Foxhole district, situated at the base of Kilvey Hill. The sides of the hill (which is 650 feet above sea level) are almost sheer in places, but towards the base are gentler slopes on which stood a row of houses. ('Time was', the *Cardiff Times and South Wales Weekly News* commented gloomily, 'when the side was covered with vegetation but the fumes from the adjacent works having killed it, there has been nothing to hold the earth together, and consequently a kind of rubble is all that keeps the rock from view.') The inhabitants of Kilvey Road and adjacent streets had often been subject to minor inundations during heavy rainfalls, but nothing like this. Great torrents of water rushed down, gouging deep channels in the hillside and carrying vast quantities of mud, gravel, stones and boulders, some of which weighed several hundredweight. The tide of water and debris burst upon the houses at the base of the hill, in some cases knocking down walls, in others forcing its way through doors and windows.

'The torrent never stopped,' it was reported, 'but bursting in the back doors and windows carried all the contents of the dwellings with it, while men, women and children were no more respected, there being cases where people were washed from a back room into a front room, out of the door, and down the hill to houses below.'

There were apparently four main torrents and several smaller ones. The first of the large streams ran down from the quarry, along Jericho Hill and, cutting away the hillside, surged along towards Canaan Chapel, which was not badly damaged although the road leading to it was covered to a depth of several feet with earth, mud and stones. The second stream came down behind Kilvey Girls' School and after flooding the building swept on to Pleasant Row. A third torrent cut a path behind houses in Kilvey Road, and a fourth hit the same road further down, these latter torrents pouring out through the front doors before uniting to advance on Pleasant Row. Ultimately the floodwaters drained away into the River Tawe.

Scenes of chaos and panic followed the inundation, shouts and screams mingling with the roar of waters as parents rushed around frantically searching for their children. A girl named Katie Lane, a fish-seller, was sheltering at the home of Mr and Mrs Samuel Brooks in Foxhole Road, with two other children, when the back door suddenly burst open and a torrent of stones, water and mud poured into the house. All managed to escape, with the exception of Katie who clung to the mantelpiece and was pinned there by the debris, screaming and in great pain for two-and-a-half hours before she was rescued and taken to hospital.

John Jones and his family had just sat down to dinner at their home in Kilvey Road when the torrent truck. He and his wife with their three children barely had time to escape before the inrush of mud and debris filled their house up to the bedroom windows. They lost nearly all they possessed, as did their next-door neighbours, Mr and Mrs Francis John.

A few doors away in Kilvey Road, William Jones was standing waiting for the storm to pass before going out; suddenly the torrent struck, smashing down the doors, coursing through the house and depositing four feet of sand on the kitchen floor. Frederick Weedon's house in Pleasant Row was similarly wrecked by the impact of the water and boulders which burst in through the back door, but he managed to get his eleven children upstairs where they were later taken out through the bedroom windows. The *Cardiff Times* reported:

A great number of houses were blocked up from floor to ceiling with dirt and great boulders, while in Foxhole Road and Kilvey Road was one continuous heap of earth quite six feet deep. It is useless to particularise houses which have suffered, as in nearly all instances the circumstances are almost precisely alike. Everything had been spoiled, while clothes and victuals were washed away by the torrent. One old man had managed to save £25 in an old stocking, and every halfpenny was washed away. Others have lost jewellery. This disastrous flood will be the more seriously felt

because all the sufferers are working men. Help is greatly needed,
for much misery and destitution prevail.

All this devastation occurred in the space of half an hour, and left
the community in Foxhole shocked and dazed. However, the chief
constable, Captain Colquhoun, and the mayor, Mr Rees, were
soon on the scene and they organized the distribution of food and
arranged shelter for those who had been forced out of their homes.
Captain Colquhoun later purchased clothes for thirty-eight
children who were clad in little more than rags. The following
morning, hundreds of men, under the supervision of Mr Wyrill,
the borough engineer, began to clear the debris, 400 cartloads
were taken away by ten o'clock. The total reached 1,000 cartloads
within a few days and the debris was used to fill a hollow where a
new stretch of railway line was being constructed. Deep gullies had
been cut into the hillside by the torrents of water, and drains were
damaged, and sometimes exposed, after several feet of topsoil had
been scoured away. Generally speaking, there was little structural
damage to houses, but furniture and fittings were ruined and many
personal belongings lost. The flood was a terrible blow to the poor
and a relief fund was organized to provide all possible help.

On the following Tuesday it was decided to try to construct
culverts on the hillsides, to carry away floodwater and prevent, if
possible, such a disaster happening again. Work soon began, but
as the *Cardiff Times* pointed out: 'Had these precautions been
adopted a few months ago, when the inhabitants loudly insisted on
the necessity, much misery and ruin might have been prevented.'

What exactly had caused the deluge? Some people asserted that
a waterspout had travelled from the bay and then burst over
Kilvey Hill. Indeed one witness, a Mr Gwynne, said he had seen
the spout over the area, while a second, less certain, reported that
he had seen a 'peculiar appearance in the direction of the hill.'
However, there seems to have been general scepticism locally
regarding the waterspout theory, and one can't help thinking that
what Mr Gwynne had seen was one of those long, pendulous
columns which have been reported at the outset of other
cloudbursts.

Undoubtedly the most spectacular case of this type occurred in
1892, at the Yorkshire village of Langtoft, which enjoys a 'claim to
fame' in its connection with Peter of Langtoft (died 1307), a
scholar and 'rhyming chronicler' who wrote a history of England to
the time of Edward I, in French verse. The village is situated some
ten miles west of the coastal town of Bridlington, and is

surrounded by hills; five of the approaches to it are down hills and
the sixth is along a narrow valley. It has often suffered minor floods
in wet weather, despite the aqueducts constructed to carry excess
water away from it.

On Sunday evening, 3 July 1892, many of its population of 565
would have been preparing for church regardless of the black clouds
gathering over the Yorkshire Wolds and the threat of the deluge to
come. At about 6 p.m. Digby Cayley left the village of Cowlam
where he had spent the afternoon to return to his home at Malton,
hoping to avoid the storm. He had driven his gig for about a mile on
the Lutton Road when he saw, approaching from the west, a
particularly dense black cloud with four long columns hanging from
it (see Fig.9). The longest and darkest column seemed to descend to
within 150 feet of the ground. As Mr Cayley watched the cloud
suddenly turned towards the south-east and moved quickly towards
Cowlam, Langtoft and Driffield. He continues:

> Up to that time, although the thunder and lightning were appalling,
> no rain had fallen on me. Suddenly, there came a flash close over

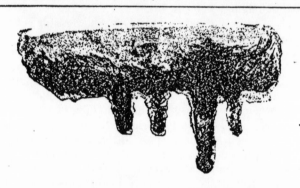

"I enclose a rough sketch of the appearance of the cloud which I have every reason to
believe caused the great damage at the
above named places.

"The cloud was decidedly blackest
nearest the longest column."

Sep. 21st. 1892.   'DIGBY CAYLEY.'

Fig.9 Mr Cayley's drawing of the black cloud over the Yorkshire Wolds

my head and a terrific peal of thunder almost at the same moment, and the next minute all was black and the water fell in bucketfulls, and the inky darkness completely hid the black cloud I had previously noticed.

His gig filled with water, which was also pouring down the road in a torrent nearly a foot deep. This, however, was nothing compared with the deluge which was soon to strike Langtoft. The storm had begun at the village at about 7 p.m. with incessant lightning, a fall of hailstones and torrential rain. By 7.20, the centre of the storm was directly over Langtoft, the water descending in sheets, every thunder-clap seeming to produce waves of water in the air. By 7.35 the storm had passed, and the sun began to shine through the clouds, but, unknown to the villagers, the columns of water that Digby Cayley had observed had burst in the surrounding hills, and raging torrents were pouring towards the village.

It seems that two of the four great columns of water burst almost simultaneously – though some distance apart – one at Woodhill near Cowlam, and the other on a hillside at Cottam. This resulted in a huge volume of water gathering in the valley leading from Cowlam to Driffield, and shortly after flooding into Driffield. The remaining part of the cloud, with its two appendages, then burst on the slopes of Round Hill about three-quarters of a mile west of Langtoft, causing the flooding there. The water had struck the hill with tremendous force, scouring away many tons of stone and chalk which was carried into the valley below, leaving huge holes in the hillside. The schoolmaster of Langtoft, Mr Bell, described how the floodwater descended on the village:

The water came in two directions, one part from Honey Hill, as it is called, and the other from Thistle Hill, along a valley called Briggate. The two streams joined at the end of Briggate, and with their united force rushed upon the village. The first thing it reached was a wall sixty or seventy yards long, and nearly six feet high, separating some gardens from the high road – it felled the wall to the ground. It then rushed upon a row of houses, twelve in number, bursting open some of the doors and carrying away a large part of the furniture. At the end of the first house the depth of the water was about seven feet. In one of these a woman nearly drowned before she could move upstairs. Had not two of her sons dragged her out she must have been lost.

The water then rushed on to the centre of the village, flooding the houses to the rear of the pond to a depth of five or six feet; one old man clung desperately to a roof until rescued, had he fallen off he would certainly have drowned; a horse tethered in a stable broke free, swimming round for a long time until, exhausted, it reached higher ground and safety; whilst pigs swam everywhere, and several drowned. The water burst into the house of Mr Woodmansey, which had already been badly damaged by lightning, filling it in an instant before forcing its way out through the back door, sweeping with it most of his furniture. It then wrecked his carpentry shop, carrying away his tools and stock of wood, before flooding another house, forcing the terrified occupants to break out through the roof. Further down the village the floodwater burst upon three two-storey chalk-built cottages, demolishing the greater part of them. The occupants of two were at chapel when the flood struck, but in the third were Mr and Mrs Stork and a friend, who took refuge in a bedroom, where they were trapped when the entire front of the house was washed away. They were eventually rescued by means of a long ladder from the other side of the street, expecting to be plunged into the torrent at any minute. There were several other narrow escapes; Mrs Gray, an eighty-year-old widow, was almost drowned when trapped by her clothing in her cottage door which had slammed shut after bursting open – she escaped by struggling out of her clothes and scrambling upstairs. In another cottage, a young woman was trapped in an upper room with her baby, her rescuers making their way along a wall at the rear of the house before breaking through the roof. Astonishingly, no one was killed by the flood, perhaps because of superhuman rescues by neighbours, and also because many were still in church or chapel when the catastrophe occurred.

The gardens, like those of most country folk a valuable source of extra food, were ruined by the flood, vegetables being uprooted or covered by a thick layer of clay-like mud. Tremendous damage was caused too on neighbouring farms, vast quantities of turnips being washed away and corn and other crops destroyed, while hedges were torn up or crushed by debris. Many acres of crops were covered by soil scoured off the surrounding hillsides; farm outbuildings were destroyed, and a threshing machine weighing four-and-a-half tons was carried forty feet across a farmyard. At a Mr Sowerby's farm, two hundred chickens were drowned and his elegantly furnished house filled with five feet of water, his wife and daughters being stranded for a while on a window-ledge as their furniture floated round. Some sixty-five houses were severely damaged by the flood.

A very touching picture is evoked by the comment of a Mr Bell, who lost furniture, books and papers when his cottage was flooded:

The poor people have been washing and scrubbing all the week and yet seem very little better. Nevertheless they appear in good heart, and are trying their best to get things set right. They are busy fetching home what they can find, such as doors, tubs, chairs, tables and a multitude of other things which have been washed along the Kilham Road. Great sympathy is being shown to the sufferers by the public, and subscriptions have been opened in various quarters, with good results.

The relief fund was initiated by the Reverend T.D.T. Speck, the vicar of Langtoft, who on Monday 4 July 1892, appealed through the newspapers for donations. He also purchased two pounds' worth of bread for the village people, and many came from surrounding districts with supplies, among them Mrs Kingston of Kilham West Field, who brought food and tea, and Mr F. Purdon and Mr Waind who arrived next day from Driffield with bacon, bread, tea and bottled water, Langtoft's water-supply from Driffield having been cut off. Over five hundred people contributed to the relief fund which reached a total of £1,340.18s.5d. Thousands of people visited Langtoft over the following week, many commenting that the destruction was worse than the newspaper reports had led them to believe.

At Driffield the effects of the flooding were not so serious, partly because several folk outside the town saw the water coming and were able to raise the alarm. The first person to realize that a flood was imminent was the manager of the waterworks, Charles Cooper, who, at about 8.00 p.m., from the elevated position of the reservoir, saw a broad stream of water coursing over the hills into the valley, in the direction of Driffield. He rushed down into the town and though he was at first met with disbelief, he was soon joined by two others, Mr Wood and Mr Highmoor, who, at about 8.15, had seen from Mr Wood's house at Kendal the water streaming along the valley. They too had rushed into the town, arriving a few minutes before the water poured into Driffield; Mr Wood remained to assist at the north end while Mr Highmoor went through the town to get the sluices and canal locks opened. This allowed much of the floodwater to be carried off by the canal and averted much damage and distress.

G.J. Symons was of the opinion that not less than *100 inches of rain* had fallen on the hillsides during the storm, which had lasted little more than half an hour. It is an astonishing figure, and other meteorologists of the day were sceptical, but the modern view is that Symons's figures were probably not far out. No rainfall stations recorded any exceptionally heavy rain in the area, again illustrating the localized nature of such deluges.

This was by no means the first time that Langtoft had suffered disastrous floods. The cataclysm of 1892 revealed a curious memorial in Mr Stork's wrecked cottage – a stone set into a wall recording an earlier inundation in 1657 (see Fig.10). By a curious coincidence the waters of the flood of 1892 just reached the stone which had evidently been placed in the wall to indicate the height of the seventeenth-century flood.

Fig.10 The inscribed stone in Mr Stork's cottage

The Round Hill seemed to act as a focus for the angry elements; in 1853, during a severe thunderstorm, three horses ploughing on the hill were killed by lightning, though the ploughmen survived; and in 1888 the hill was struck by a bursting 'waterspout' similar to those of 1892. At about one o'clock on the afternoon of 9 June 1888, an enormous column 'resembling Sir Tatton Sykes's monument turned upside down' was seen approaching the village. (The memorial to Sir Tatton Sykes is five miles north-west of Driffield on the B1252.) Where the water column burst on the hillside, it gouged out chalk, clay and flint, which it deposited in an adjoining field. The water poured into the village, though the flood was not as destructive as that which occurred four years later.

What is the explanation for such phenomenal downpours? Even today there seems to be no satisfactory answer. Meteorologists have seriously considered the possibility that they are the result of bursting waterspouts. Dr G.T. Meaden, for example, suggested that the Oxford deluge of 1682 was caused in this manner. It seems rather a clumsy explanation, however, and does not take into account all the different features of such cases. It is possible that air currents play a part in the process. The maximum speed of a raindrop falling in still air is 17 m.p.h., but if currents of air rose at a speed greater than 17 m.p.h. the rain could not fall. If, however, such air currents suddenly ceased, after holding back the rain, a tremendous accumulation of water could descend. It is possible that certain types of terrain may 'capture' and concentrate passing storm systems – it will have been noticed that most of the cases described in this chapter occurred in hilly districts – and lightning may also play a part in the sudden release of vast quantities of water. For over a century, rain gushes have been linked to lightning flashes, and C.B. Moore, after studying storms in the West Indies, wrote in the *Journal of the Atmospheric Sciences* in 1964, 'An analysis indicates that within 30 seconds after a lightning discharge, the mass of some droplets may increase as much as 100-fold as a result of an electrostatic precipitation effect.'

4   The Moray Floods

Sir Thomas Dick Lauder (1784–1848) was one of those remarkable polymaths so characteristic of nineteenth-century Britain. In 1815 he began to contribute papers on chemistry, natural history and meteorology to the *Annals of Philosophy* and in 1825 and 1827 produced two novels, respectively *Lochindhu* and *The Wolf of Badenoch*, which were enormously popular. As secretary to the Royal Institution for the Encouragement of the Fine Arts, he devoted much energy to the foundation of art and technical schools and produced several works describing the natural history, antiquities, geology and geography of Scotland.

It is to Sir Thomas that we owe most of our knowledge of the floods which devastated the county of Moray in August 1829; he had been prevailed upon to write a history of the floods by Lord Cockburn, who had visited Lauder's estate, Relugas, which had itself suffered greatly during the flood. Sir Thomas travelled round the county, meticulously recording details, not merely of the flood itself, but of the region's folklore, history, dialect and geography, thus giving a remarkable picture of Moray as it was 160 years ago.

The months of May, June and July 1829 were exceptionally dry, with the drought occasionally being interrupted by sudden downpours. These falls of rain became heavier and more frequent as the summer continued, reaching a climax on the 3rd and 4th of August, when 3¾ inches of rain, about one-sixth of the county's annual rainfall, fell in a twenty-four hour period. (This figure was recorded at Huntly Lodge on the Duke of Gordon's estate, between 5 a.m. Monday the 3rd, and 5 a.m. the following morning.) Most of the rain fell on the Monadhliath mountains, and on the Cairngorms, the rivers Nairn, Findhorn and Lossie, and their tributaries, becoming raging torrents which battered down bridges, washed away houses, flooded vast areas of farmland and in many places completely altered the appearance of the landscape.

As mentioned above, great destruction was caused at Sir

Thomas's estate, situated on the edge of Darnaway Forest, bounded to the west by the Findhorn and to the north and east by the Divie. On the evening of 3 August Lauder was called, while at dinner, by his servants, alarmed by the swollen condition of the rivers. Despite the torrential rain and a howling gale he went outside, later reporting that:

> ...the Divie appalled us! Looking up its source to where it burst from the rocks it resembled the outlet to some great inland sea, that had suddenly broken from its bounds. It was already 8 or 10 feet higher than anyone had ever seen it, and setting directly down against the sloping terrace under the offices, where we were standing, it washed up over the shrubs and strawberry beds, with a strange and alarming flux and re-flux, dashing out over the ground 10 or 15 yards at a time – covering the knees of some of the party, standing, as they thought, far beyond its reach – and retreating with a suction which it required great exertion to resist.

The noise was tremendous: a continual uniform roar from the rushing waters augmented by repeated reports, resembling cannon fire and caused apparently by the rolling along of great boulders on the rocky bed of the Divie. Above all this was the shrieking of the gale, which caused the trees to bend and crack and stripped the leaves from their branches. Sir Thomas described in detail, and with great sadness, the destruction at Relugas. A magnificent group of trees, 'well known friends,' which stood on the Mill Island in the Divie were toppled over one after another and carried away by the river; a small Doric temple, raised on an isolated rock close to the island was swept away, as were several ornamental bridges, and the river banks, covered with a luxuriant growth of laurels, rhododendrons, azaleas, lilacs and roses, were scoured away to the bare rock. By the morning, the Mill Island, formerly separated from the river bank on one side by a small stream, was in the middle of a wide channel, the swollen river flowing majestically along. The gentle slopes of the river-banks on either side of the island were cut right back, leaving on one side a precipice fifty feet high, the base of which was being relentlessly cut away by the river – great chunks of ground, some surmounted by trees periodically tumbling into the water. The damage at Relugas, writes Lauder, was in value about £1,200 but this mattered little in relation to the loss of the beautiful scenery. 'Never,' he wrote, 'did the unsubstantiality of all earthly things come so perfectly home to my conviction.' Sir Thomas never felt the same about Relugas, it seems, after the flood, for he left there shortly after, to reside in the old family mansion of The Grange, near Edinburgh.

Great destruction was also caused on the estate of Dunphail about 1½ miles from Relugas which belonged to Mr Cummings Bruce, and on the Monday evening the water had begun to approach the house itself. The mansion, only recently built, was situated on a wide lawn, about fifty feet from an old channel, which remained dry except during the time of floods, with the River Divie running along a steep wooded bank, bounding the valley to the west, about six hundred feet from the house. The space in between was occupied by a raised, partially wooded, island, on which grazed a 27-year-old pony, Dobbin, a much loved pet, resembling, the family said, 'a 74-gun ship cut down to a frigate'. At about six o'clock the river carried away two wooden bridges, one for carriages and the other for pedestrians, and washed away an embankment at the upper end of the island, causing a great torrent to pour down the channel in front of the house. The water began to scour away the land and Mr Bruce, seeing that the house was threatened, evacuated his wife and daughter by carriage to a friend's house. Everyone was now extremely anxious about the fate of Dobbin, who was stranded on the island (floodwaters never having risen so high before, no one had thought to remove him.). He was seen galloping frantically to and fro, as trees and debris floated past him, then, as the last remaining patch of land disappeared he plunged into the water. He rose and sank several times, actually being turned head over heels by the force of the torrent, and finally, when everyone believed he had gone, he emerged from the water and scrambled to safety.

After he had left the ladies in safety, Mr Bruce returned to Dunphail at about ten o'clock to find the flood had undermined the bank to within a few paces of the foundation of the kitchen tower and watched, horrified, as great chunks of land, surmounted by fine trees more than a century old, toppled into the water. At eleven o'clock the space between the house and the flood was three yards and still the waters rose. Mr Bruce, considering his home lost, reluctantly ordered the furniture to be removed and by the light of lanterns the contents of the house were carried out. About one o'clock on the Tuesday morning the flood subsided slightly, but in an hour the waters rose again and the bank was washed away *to within a yard of the house*. Mr Bruce now ordered everyone to move to a safe distance from the doomed mansion, and they all prepared to watch its destruction. At about four

Fig. 11. Mr Cummings Bruce's house after the waters had receded

o'clock, however, the waters again began to recede, and this time there was no resurgence. A sloping beach slowly became visible as the water went down, and Mr Bruce realized that his house was safe (Fig.11).

The flood brought ruin to many small farmers, Sir Thomas wrote, after a journey along the banks of the Findhorn:

> It was melancholy to behold the devastation committed by the flood on every little farm we passed, some of which were really altogether ruined by the annihilation of their arable land. That of Dallas, for instance, lost no less than 17 acres. The river having filled the glen from side to side, the whole crop in the bottom was necessarily destroyed, and misery and wretchedness everywhere.

One of the farmers was William Fraser whose house on the level land beside the Findhorn began to fill with water on the Monday evening. He and his brother quickly brought out their sister and their aged mother, and then retreated to higher ground. They had no sooner reached safety than their house and outbuildings were swallowed up by the flood. The Frasers managed to rescue their cattle, but their crops were ruined, five or six acres of arable land had been carried away, and the rest of their farmland was covered with deep deposits of sand and gravel. All that remained of their buildings was the end of a cowhouse.

William Sutherland of Dunphail had laboured hard to build a carding- and meal-mill on the banks of the Dorback, immediately above a point where the glen narrows before joining the valley of the Divie. About eighteen months previously Sir Thomas had been to inspect the newly built mill and, highly impressed by the young man's achievement, sent a report to the Board of Trustees for the Encouragement of Scottish Manufacturers, who had given him a handsome payment. On the afternoon of 3 August the millrace had been flooded by the Dorback, causing a wide stream to cut off the dwelling house from the bank. It was too deep to ford and William Sutherland and his family, his pony, pigs and cows, were cut off. After a temporary subsidence the flood began to rise again, the water pouring in through the doors and windows. The miller ran to fetch his young brother from his bed and took him to the meal-mill where the elevated floor was still dry. By this time the cattle and pigs were up to their bellies in water, so William thrust several big bundles of straw under them to raise them up. He had just returned to the house when the south gable, against which the water had been beating, crashed in, and he had quickly to throw open the window in the opposite wall to let the rushing water out. It was a terrifying ordeal for the family. The waves were as high as the house, and enormous trees were being carried down by the river and smashed against the buildings. At five o'clock the miller saw his neighbours, the Grants, watching from the far bank of the river about thirty yards away, but the roar of the water prevented any communication, and to Sutherland's despair they departed. He continued:

> Every moment we expected the crazed walls of the house to yield, and to bury us in the ruins, or that we and it together should be swept away. We began to prepare ourselves for the fate that awaited us. I thank Almighty God that supported me in that hour of trial. I felt calm and collected, and my assistant was no less so. My little brother, too, said 'he was na feared', but the woman and the lad were frantic, and did nothing but shriek and wring their hands.

Happily, though, rescue was at hand. The Grants had now returned to the riverbank with a crowd of about sixty people and several lengths of rope. A post was driven into the bank of the river and one end of a rope attached, the other end being successfully thrown across to the mill, where it was tied to a strong beam. Another rope was then thrown across and one end attached to the little boy's waist. He was then pulled through the water to the bank, supporting himself as he went on the fixed rope. In this manner the whole family was taken safely from the island. It was the end of the miller's livelihood, however, as the foundations of the buildings were undermined, the walls thrown down, a deep ravine gouged out between the island and the bank, the machinery destroyed and the whole layout of the land altered. It was quite impossible for a mill to be built there again, by Sutherland or anyone.

John Grant, a shoemaker who lived near the Bridge of Nevie on the River Livat, had the centre of his house entirely washed away by the river which burst its banks on the evening of 3 August. He, his wife, four children and his apprentice were saved but his account-books, and furniture, were swept away. The Grants sought refuge at the nearby house of Alexander Innes, but the flood pursued them there, and both families had to flee for their lives. Mr Innes, anxious to retrieve some papers, insisted on returning to the house, but on leaving again he was submerged by a tremendous torrent of water, and would have drowned but for two blacksmiths who immediately plunged in and dragged him to safety. When danger had passed John Grant erected a makeshift shelter at one end of his ruined cottage, the remnants of his furniture being piled on the heaps of sand that had half-buried the ruined building, but it is pleasant to record that his neighbours built a fine new stone cottage for him, at a safe distance from the river.

The village of Dallas was flooded at about five o'clock on the morning of 4 August, the water from the River Lossie filling the houses to a depth of three feet in a matter of minutes. Scenes of the utmost confusion followed: women and children were taken out of windows, horses and carts pressed into service, and the elderly and infirm carried through the streets on men's shoulders. Most of the people were taken to the church which was situated on higher ground. One hundred and twenty people were safely evacuated, due in no small measure to the efforts of one local man, 'Quarry Jock', a strong and capable character who seems to have established some sort of order in the situation. The following evening Kenneth Maclean, a blacksmith, returned to the village, anxious for the safety of his pregnant sow, and was nearly drowned before being pulled from the torrent by the local shoemaker, James Edwards. Cold and dripping, Maclean nevertheless managed to save his animal, taking her upstairs to his own bedroom where, shortly after, she gave birth to a fine litter of piglets! The villagers suffered greatly; their houses were filled with sand and mud, their furniture swept away, crops destroyed and their entire stocks of winter fuel carried away. The water continued to flow through the village until a protective bulwark was built on 5 August. The large farm attached to the Mill of Dallas was also devastated, the river carving a completely new channel through one of the finest parts of the land, and tremendous damage was caused on Sir William Cummings's estate, above the church of Dallas.

Another hasty evacuation occurred at Garmouth on the River Spey where the inhabitants had ignored warnings of the impending flood and gone to bed as usual. While they slept the water began to flow into the town, the houses in the lower part of Garmouth being deeply flooded by midnight. Many people, awakened by the commotion, jumped out of bed to find themselves knee-deep in water, their furniture floating around them. At 2.30 there was a great rumble as a building toppled into the water, the noise being repeated with horrible regularity as others followed. The sound was accompanied by rumbling of carts, the roaring of the flood, the splashing of ceaseless rain and shouts and screams of frightened people. Men waded waist-deep through the streets, carrying women, children, the elderly and infirm. Eight dwelling houses and seven other buildings were destroyed by the flood and virtually every house in the lower part of the town was damaged. Opposite the saw-mill at Garmouth the water rose to ten feet above its normal level and the inundation was no less than a mile across. Sir Thomas Lauder later wrote:

> When I visited Garmouth, I beheld many houses of two, and even three storeys, half thrown down, with the nicely painted walls and ceilings of what were snug and comfortable rooms, now laid open perpendicularly, and appearing tier above tier. But what must have been the spectacle, when day dawned on the 4th of August, while torrents still filled the streets, and the extent of that night's destruction was revealed?

It is recorded that great kindness was displayed by the more fortunate inhabitants of Garmouth to those who had been forced out of their homes, one Captain Fyfe inviting all destitute individuals and families into his home without discrimination, and providing them with food, warmth and shelter.

Many bridges were destroyed by the swollen rivers though it was the older structures, curiously, that often survived, such as that over the Nairn at Kilravock, which 'resisted the flood like a veteran warrior'. The older bridges usually had steep ascents from each side towards the centre, and during flooding the water escaped over the low ends. When bridges were modernized by having the approaches built up, and the roads raised, the floodwater had no escape route, and was forced through arches inadequate to contain it, which gave way under the pressure. One of the bridges destroyed by the flood was that over the Divie, immediately above the point where it was joined by the Dorback, a handsome structure of a single arch which had stood for the better part of a century. When the floodwater broke right over the parapets of the bridge it withstood the pressure for a quarter of an hour before some large trees were carried down and, trapped by the bridge, dammed the waters behind them. Finally, the pressure became too great and the bridge was carried away *en masse*, actually travelling for some distance before disintegrating. Of this Sir Thomas wrote: 'The extraordinary fact was established by the evidence of an eyewitness, whose testimony is unquestionable; nor was this a solitary instance of so wonderful a proof of the power of the flood.' Also notable was the destruction of the Bridge of Curr, over the River Dulnain, another single-arch structure with a span of sixty-five feet. The southern abutment of the bridge was undermined by the water, a witness asserting that the instant the

support gave way, the force of the water was so great as to make
the arch spring fifteen feet into the air and that while ascending it
kept its perfect semicircular form.

The bridge at Fochabers, over the River Spey, had four arches,
two of ninety-five feet and two of seventy-five feet. The view from
it on the morning of the 4th presented a vast expanse of dark
brown water, from the base of Benagen Hill on one side to the sea
on the other, a distance of some ten miles. The river was two miles
wide in places and dotted here and there with evidence of the
flood's destruction: the tops of submerged trees, roofs of houses to
which, in some cases, the inhabitants clung, awaiting rescue by the
many small boats which were busy in the river, and all manner of
floating debris. By eight o'clock that morning the floodwaters
were seventeen feet above normal at the bridge and many people
went on to it to view the wreckage and animal carcases floating
down, and the boiling, swirling waters round the piers. It was on
this bridge that one of the fatalities occurred. At about 12.20 p.m.
Gordon Macewan, a teacher at Fochabers, was crossing with
several others when he saw a crack suddenly appear on the bridge
in front of them. 'Good God!', he cried, 'the bridge is falling; run
for your lives!' He and several others managed to leap to safety as
two arches of the bridge plunged into the water. One of the men,
William Sivewright, a mason, later described what happened:

> ...the parapet wall folded round before me and parted from the
> roadway, which then seemed whole; but, ere I had time to cry out,
> it was falling in a thousand pieces, cracking endlong and across from
> the centre. I sprang sideways past Anderson and Cuthbert, and
> leaped from fragment to fragment of the falling roadway, as if I had
> been flying. When I reached the rock I was blind for a moment;
> and, when I recovered and looked round, Anderson and Cuthbert
> were gone.

John Cuthbert managed to climb to safety after the road gave way
beneath his feet, but John Anderson, after making a futile effort to
grab Cuthbert's coat, fell down amongst the rubble of the bridge.
His body was found that evening, about a mile downstream,
entangled with driftwood.

A remarkable sight was witnessed from the bridge over the
River Nethy at the settlement called Bridge of Nethy, before it too
succumbed to the floodwaters. About eight o'clock on the morning
of 4 August a crowd on the bridge were watching the swirling river
as it tossed great trees about, when the sawmill of Straanbeg,

about five hundred yards up river, a huge timber building, was carried off:

> ...steadily and magnificently, like some three decker leaving dock. On it came grandly, with not a plank being dislodged. It was tremendous – it was awful to see it advancing on the bridge. The people shuddered. Some moved quickly away, and others, spellbound, instinctively grasped the parapet to prepare for the shock: its speed was accelerated, it was already within 100 yards, and the increased velocity of the current must bring it instantaneously upon them; destruction seemed inevitable, when all at once it struck upon a bulwark, went to pieces with a fearful crash, and spreading itself abroad all over the surface of the waters, it rushed down to the Spey in one sea of wreck.

The bridge itself, of granite with a central arch of thirty-six feet and two side arches of twenty-four feet, had its western arch washed away by the flood.

Also destroyed was the elegant stone bridge of five arches, constructed by Thomas Telford over the Dee at Ballater. At about 3.30 on the afternoon of 4 August, the two northern arches of the bridge were swept away, to be followed over the next two hours by the remaining three. The wind and rain of the previous day had been accompanied at Ballater by violent thunder and lightning and, curiously, according to several people, by an earthquake. An earthquake was also reported at Strathdon, by Mr Watson, the landlord of the New Arms Inn. He was awakened between one and two o'clock on the morning of the 4th by the tremor, and though he could not tell its direction he said that it shook all the glasses and tumblers in his cupboards and threw down a clock key which was placed on top of the clock-case. The schoolhouse at Strathdon was also shaken.

One of the most bizarre incidents of the disaster occurred at a small lake called Loch-na-mhoon near Avielochan, about 2½ miles to the north of Aviemore. The loch lay in a hollow and was about ninety yards in length and fifty in width. The centre of it was occupied by a swampy, roughly circular, island, about thirty yards across, which rose and fell with the surface of the water. It was composed of *Eriophori, Junci* and other water plants, their matted roots, about eighteen inches long, attached to a great mass of soil, some eighteen inches thick, thus giving the solid part of the island a thickness of some three feet. During the flood:

... one of the cross drains of the road sent a stream directly down a hollow, and rushed into the loch with so great a force that it actually undermined and tore up the island; and the surface of the water being thus raised 15 or 20 feet, and the wind blowing furiously from the north-east, the huge mass was floated and drifted to the southern shore, and stranded on the steep bank, where it now lies like a great carpet, the upper half of it reclining on the slope of the bank, and the lower half resting on the more level ground close to the water's edge.

A remarkable incident occurred on the banks of the River Dorback. A hill about a hundred feet high, planted with birch and alder trees, became so soaked with the rain that it began to disintegrate, and a gigantic mass, about an acre in extent, gave way and slid downwards, blocking the swollen river. This was witnessed by William Macdonald, the farmer at Easter Tillyglens, who told Lauder that it fell with 'a sort o' dumb sound' which, commented Sir Thomas, 'although somewhat of a contradiction in terms, will yet convey the true meaning better than any more correct expression.' The farmer continued to stare as the floodwaters built up behind the natural dam, till about an hour later the pressure became too great and the gigantic mass gave way and was swept along like a floating island. As Macdonald watched, dumbfounded, a further half-acre of land, with a grove of trees on it, detached itself from the hill and descended into the river. The floodwaters tore at the mass, gradually breaking it up and carrying it away, but part of it remained, with trees growing in an upright position, having travelled sixty or seventy yards.

Another strange occurrence was that witnessed from the road to Ballindalloch, which winds round the northern base of the isolated hill of Tomanurd, an outpost of the Cromdale mountains. On Tuesday 4 August, a Mr Grant of Culquoich was walking past the hill when there was a tremendous quaking of the earth for approximately sixty or seventy yards above the road, and an immense column of water burst through the hillside, spouting high into the air and carrying stones, gravel and chunks of earth. Huge chunks of the hillside were thrown for a distance of up to three hundred yards around. Sometimes the spout would cease and then burst forth again like a geyser. Sir Thomas visited the spot a few days after with a friend, a civil engineer, and they calculated that no less than 7,000 cubic yards of earth had been moved. A tiny trickle of water was all that flowed from the ravine now, however. Lauder could only conclude that the hill had contained an underground reservoir which was augmented to bursting point by the heavy rain.

The west side of the River Findhorn was the scene of many remarkable stories of tragedy, heroism and survival. Here the well-to-do Mr Suter of Moy House and his friend Dr Brand played an active role in superhuman attempts of the cottage folk to rescue their neighbours and friends, as well as opening Moy House to all in need of food, warmth and shelter.

On his way to dine with his friend on Monday 3 August, Dr Brand's horse had almost been swept away by the river in spate and rising rapidly. After dining, the two men went out to spread the warning and persuade as many families as they could to leave their houses for shelter on safer ground. Mostly their advice was heeded, but the Kerr family felt they were at a safe distance from the river and remained in their home. The men returned to Moy House, but about ten o'clock as they were sitting in an upstairs room a young servant boy rushed in and cried 'The Findhorn's rolling by the square, Sir! There's a heap o' houses down at the Broom of Moy and four or five fouk drowned, and a' the rest of them is in the kitchen, Sir!' The men rushed down and found a group of dripping, shivering women and children round the blazing fire: knocking was heard at the door and in walked one Andrew Smith, with a child in his arms, and his wife and seven more children. He told them that several people were trapped in the floodwater, including Sandy Smith, a popular local boatman, and his family, the site of whose cottage was particularly vulnerable. Hurrying outside they saw a gleam of light coming from the dwelling, 'I have often heard of a ray of hope,' said Mr Suter, 'but this is the first time I have experienced it in a literal sense!'

The men joined a group in a nearby field, who were scanning the floodwater, anxious also for the safety of the Kerr family, now trapped in their cottage, but all attention was suddenly diverted by loud cries coming from the gardener's wife and his children trapped in their cottage near the estate offices. Hurrying across, Mr Suter found water swirling round the house and began to wade across. He was immediately joined by Mrs Ross, his washerwoman, who exclaimed, 'God forbid that ye should risk yourself alane, Sir!' and joined him in the water. The pair were soon up to their waists, the woman, more familiar with the ground, acting as guide. They reached the cottage door and the gardener's youngest son jumped happily on to Mr Suter's back; within ten minutes the whole family had been saved.

Cattle, sheep and horses had been gathered from adjacent farms and making his way up to the Black Barn Mr Suter found many had taken refuge there. Most of the women and children were sent up to the house for the night, and on his return he found no fewer than thirteen children in his kitchen, eating broth from a great wooden dish. He ordered that candles should be placed in the windows, so that Sandy Smith and his family could see and take heart from them, and then retired for the night.

At daybreak all they could see was a vast swirling brownish-yellow stretch of water, dotted here and there with treetops and covered with wreckage. The roof of Sandy Smith's cottage was visible, but the fate of the Kerr family was still unknown. Mr Kerr's son, Alexander, who was in service at Mr Suter's house, had watched all night, staring towards his home at Stripeside, but even as Mr Suter was seeking to reassure him they saw the gable of the cottage collapse. Dr Brand, however, peering through a telescope, saw a hand thrust through the thatch of the roof, followed by a head and then finally the whole of Mr Kerr's body, followed by those of his wife and niece. The family crawled slowly along the roof and then dropped down on to a small patch of dry ground at the rear of the building. For the moment they were safe, but there was hardly room for them to move. Dr Brand and Alexander Shaw, Mr Kerr's nephew, set out to search for a boat, and meanwhile with the telescope Mr Suter located Sandy and his family, who were gathered on a small patch of land, a few feet square, near their flooded cottage. Mrs Smith was sitting on a log, covered with a blanket and holding a child in her lap. Her seventeen-year-old daughter and twelve-year-old son were huddled against her. Farm animals were standing in the shallows or swimming in the water. Their position looked bleak, but as he watched Mr Suter saw that a boat had been launched at Barnhill, about a mile away. On its way though, it was diverted to rescue another family through the window of a cottage, and these were put down in a place of safety before the boat set out again, manned by Donald Munro, Sergeant John Grant (a pensioner from Findhorn) and Robert Dallas. Mr Suter said later that he would never forget the strength and bravery of Donald Munro, who, because of his dress that day, was known ever after as Yellow Waistcoat. They rowed towards the Kerrs, now left with only a few feet of ground on which to stand. It was a difficult and dangerous business, with the big waves and strong currents in the floodwaters, but finally they were picked up, Yellow Waistcoat also pulled a huge hog from the water and tossed it like a rabbit into the boat. Once they were safely among their relatives and friends, Yellow Waistcoat and his crew set out again, this time to the rescue of three elderly women, one bedridden, who were trapped in an isolated cottage, one wall of which had already given way. The boat was rowed up to the cottage where the old ladies were sitting in chairs, immersed in the water and nearly dead with cold – rescue had come in the nick of time and they were quickly taken to safety. Mr Suter dealt out whisky to the rescuers, but the old sergeant when offered a second glass replied, 'Na, I thank ye Sir, I like it ower weel: and if I tak' it I may forget mysel' and God kens we need to ha'e our wits aboot us the day.'

There was still great anxiety about poor Sandy Smith and his family, and Yellow Waistcoat and three other rescuers set out again, this time nearly losing their own lives when their boat plunged over a cataract and they were thrown into the flood. Regaining their boat by a miracle, they were swept downstream in the swirling current until they reached a spot where Sandy Smith himself had waded in to help them. Soon they were all safely on board and taken back to Moy House, where the youngest daughter joined five other bairns in one of Mrs Suter's beds. At one stage she had been unconscious, but warmth, hot broth and a good night's sleep was all she needed. Later Sandy reported:

> It was an awfu' thing to be expectin' every minute to be swept into eternity, in sic an unprepared state, and our ears driven deaf wi' the roarin' o' the waters, an' the crashin' o' the great trees that cam' bommin' past us ilka minute; an' a' thing dark aboot us, an' neething to be seen but the far distant glimmer o' Maister Suter's candles. But their light was some little comfort. It seemed as the Lord hadna' just a'thegither forsaken us.

There were other incredible rescues. In all, eight people lost their lives in the flood, a low figure perhaps considering the scale of the disaster, but many more lost their homes, their livelihoods, their savings – indeed everything they possessed. The inhabitants of Moray had only just begun to rebuild their lives when there was a further flood on 17 August which caused more destruction, though this second one was not nearly so destructive as the first. The Moray people seemed to face the floods with great dignity and stoicism. A relief fund was organized and £1,470 raised. £20 was set aside for rewards to the boatmen of the Findhorn and the Spey who had risked their lives, and £20 for various expenses, leaving the balance to be distributed amongst the neediest sufferers.

5 East Coast Inundation, 1953

> The sea in dense darkness began to be agitated by the violence of
> the wind and burst through its accustomed limits, overwhelming
> towns, fields and inundating parts which no age in past time had
> recorded to be covered in water. For issuing forth about the middle
> of the night, it suffocated or drowned men and women sleeping in
> their beds, with infants in their cradles, and many types of livestock.

This was written in 1287 by John Oxnead and described a flood
caused by the sea bursting through the Horsey Gap in Norfolk,
one of the many disastrous coastal inundations suffered by the
inhabitants of England's east coast towns over the centuries. This
particular inundation, it is thought, flooded the medieval peat
workings, and left us the legacy of the Norfolk Broads. John
Oxnead's phrase 'agitated by the violence of the wind' identified
the cause of these coastal floods, for they occur when an
exceptionally strong wind from north-west to north-east blows
down the full length of the North Sea and coincides with a spring
tide (spring, in this context, does not refer to the season but is
derived from an old Norse word 'spreng' meaning swollen or
enlarged) to form a storm surge, the result of which may be a tide
ten feet higher than normal.

In Holinshed's *Chronicle* (1577) is a description of the storm
surge of 5 October, 1571, which caused immense devastation, a
story taken up nearly three hundred years later by Jean Ingelow in
her poem 'The High Tide on the Coast of Lincolnshire (1571)' in
lines which could equally well describe the east coast tragedy
which was to follow in 1953. Of the swiftness of the engulfing tide
she wrote –

> The heart had hardly time to beat,
> Before a shallow seething wave
> Sobbed in the grasses at oure feet:
> The feet had hardly time to flee
> Before it brake against the knee,
> And all the world was in the sea.

On 31 January 1953, a surge swept down the North Sea overwhelming sea defences from Yorkshire to Kent and killing more than three hundred people. This was one of Britain's worst natural disasters, yet elsewhere in the country it seems to have been strangely forgotten. That it remains a painful and unforgettable memory for the inhabitants of east coast towns, however, was demostrated when I sought information through local newspapers. Letters arrived from places as far apart as North Lincolnshire to Canvey Island and Purfleet in the Thames Estuary, from writers of all ages, some now very old and others much younger, just children at the time. They told stories of tragedy and heroism, resourcefulness, endurance and bravery. Even today, some thirty-seven years later, some said that past events are often referred to as 'before the floods' or 'after the floods.' The experiences of some of the flood victims are described in more detail later in this chapter, but the meteorological background to the disaster is interesting.

During Friday 30 January 1953, a deep depression moved from Iceland in a south-easterly direction, gale force winds striking the north coast of Scotland late that night. Next morning the average wind speed at the Orkneys between 9.30 and 10.30 was 90 m.p.h. with gusts of up to 125 m.p.h. The gale forced a tremendous volume of Atlantic water, estimated at more than 4 billion cubic yards, southwards into the North Sea, coinciding with a spring tide and raising it ten feet above normal. Perhaps the first indication of the disaster to come, though it was not recognized as such, occurred at Aberdeen as early as 2.10 p.m. that Saturday, when the high tide rose about 2½ feet above the predicted level. As the great tide rolled further south, into the ever-narrowing bottleneck of the North Sea, the water rose higher and higher. At 3.30 p.m. the River Tees began to overflow its banks and at 5.25 the sea broke through the sandhills at Sandilands, on the Lincolnshire coast. The first disastrous flooding occurred at 7.10 p.m. with the bursting of the sea defences opposite the police station on Mablethorpe sea-front, the water pouring into the town centre. Six thousand people had to be evacuated from the coastal strip between Mablethorpe and Sutton-on-Sea; sixteen people were drowned and twenty more perished in the Skegness area. Shortly after, about 7.30 p.m. the sea defences on the north coast of Norfolk were overwhelmed, fifteen being drowned in King's Lynn and a further sixty-five between King's Lynn and Hunstanton. At 11.00 p.m. the sea-walls at Yarmouth were breached, 3,500 homes in the Southtown district were flooded, necessitating large-scale evacuation, and ten people were drowned. The tide reached its highest point during the night, and complaints were later voiced that warnings were not passed from Lincolnshire and Norfolk to Suffolk and Essex. Perhaps this was because the more northerly towns, overwhelmed as the catastrophe hit them, were battling for their own survival, and also because many telephone lines were down. For whatever reason, it appears that warning messages, which could perhaps have saved many lives, were not passed to towns further south, of the disaster sweeping towards them.

At 12.30 a.m. on Sunday 1 February the water flowed into the port of Harwich, the flood extending from the sea front to the town centre; 1,200 homes were flooded, more than fifteen hundred were made homeless and eight were drowned, while at nearby Felixstowe forty people lost their lives. At 1.45 a.m. the floods poured into Clacton-on-Sea, drowning thirty-five on the Jaywick housing estate. Sweeping into the Thames, the surge swamped Canvey Island, which (like Jaywick) had many lightly built holiday bungalows and chalets. At Canvey the death toll was fifty-eight, and 10,000 were left homeless. Millions of gallons of water poured into the streets in parts of the densely populated West Ham, flooding 1,100 homes, when approximately 100 yards of a riverside embankment was demolished, while the industrial complex of south-west Essex suffered enormous damage, oil refineries, cement works, factories, gasworks and power-stations being brought to a standstill. Damage was also extensive on the south side of the Thames: BP's oil refinery on the Isle of Grain was flooded, as was the Naval Dockyard at Sheerness, where two ships were sunk. The tidal surge finally lost its momentum between Westminster and Chelsea, just below the top of the embankment. This was the highest recorded tide in London, and a further disaster here was averted by a matter of inches.

This, then, was the path of the surge, with its toll of deaths. The terror of that night comes out in the stories I received. I am able here to describe the experiences of only a very few people, but from these one can see that it would be almost impossible to exaggerate the misery and horror of the east coast floods of 1953.

Lincolnshire.
One correspondent, Raymond Hyde, from North Hykeham near Lincoln, actually saw the sea-wall, near Mablethorpe, collapse that Saturday evening. He was twenty-three years old at the time, and living with his parents on a farm about a mile from Sutton-on-Sea. A keen motor-cyclist, Mr Hyde and his friend

John, set out that evening to ride to Mablethorpe, which is about two miles north of Sutton, having seen the water at Sutton beginning to come over the sea-wall at about 4 p.m. They got to within half a mile of Mablethorpe when the water stopped their machines, luckily as it turned out, for they then heard a tremendous roar above the sound of the wind and waves. Before their eyes, about fifty yards away, the sea-walls and sand-hills simply collapsed. The sea swept across the road, carrying telegraph-poles and streetlamps before it, into a caravan park, the caravans bouncing, Mr Hyde recalled, like ping-pong balls. Horrified at what they had seen, the two friends turned their motor-cycles round and waded with them to Trusthorpe, a village between Sutton and Mablethorpe, where they left their bikes near the church hall and knocked at a nearby house. As the door was opened the floodwater poured in – the owner and his family had heard nothing over the sound of the wind and waves and were aghast at the sight of the water coming over the sand-hills and the gigantic waves smashing the sea-wall to pieces, throwing huge

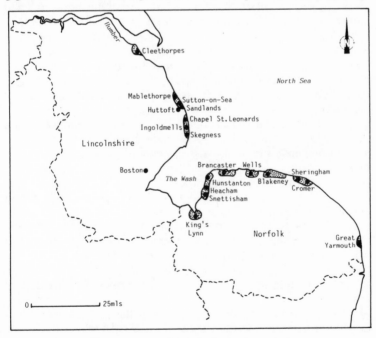

Fig. 12. Areas of Lincolnshire and Norfolk
affected by the floods of 1953

chunks of concrete into the air. Raymond and John left their motor-cycles in the family's garage and set out to walk across the fields, to get as far inland as possible. They were soon in trouble, however, for the water in places was waist-deep, making walking almost impossible. Luckily though, they were seen by a man in a nearby bungalow, built on slightly higher ground, who was trying to persuade his dogs swimming around the garden to come into the house. He called the young men inside to where a welcoming fire was blazing, and gave them hot drinks, but the water was still rising so the two young men helped their host move his carpets and furniture up into the loft. The floodwaters soon began to pour into the house, extinguishing the fire, and quickly reaching the level of the window-sills. The three men spent the rest of the night perched precariously on the table, with the hatch to the loft open above them, until the early hours of the next morning when the tide began to ebb and the water level to fall.

When daylight came and the level was low enough, Raymond and John left the bungalow and made their way back to the house at Trusthorpe to collect their bikes. They found the family had fled and the whole area was deserted, so pushing their machines they made for John's home further inland, where presumably the water would be lower and John's father could possibly drive Raymond home in the car, but it proved too deep for that so he borrowed a push-bike and set out alone. By now, though, the tide had turned again and the floodwater was rising once more and soon all he could do was to lean on the bike for support and feel for the road with his feet. The area was completely covered by sea-water and the only indications of the course of the road were the tall reeds which grew each side and the occasional high hedgerow. It took him three hours, fighting against the wind and water, to make the two mile journey home. Everywhere was deserted, he passed four houses on his way and saw no signs of life, a fact which he found curiously depressing.

Raymond's first action on reaching the farm was to free the family's dog which had dragged his kennel along by its chain, and was now trapped in the top of the hedge. He walked into the flooded kitchen, the dog swimming behind him, to find the furniture floating in about three feet of water. His parents and grandmother were in one of the bedrooms where they had managed to light a fire in the grate. On the previous evening a neighbour had called to warn them of the flood and they had taken whatever they could, including food and fuel, upstairs. Naturally they were overjoyed to see Raymond. Mr Hyde concludes:

After things had dried out somewhat my father and I got our waders on and went to see what stock had survived. The twenty cows were standing in water up to the tops of their legs so we fed them and gave them drinking water. The horse was standing in a field on a high spot in about a foot of water. He rushed to us when we opened the gates and then went to the haystack – he must have been starving. We didn't find our two farm cats for over a week, they must have been in the rafters of the barn. Our eight hundred chickens and twenty pigs were all dead. The army were moving people out by Wednesday, my mother and grandmother being taken by a DUKW to Alford where they stayed several weeks. I was among many who went to help fill sandbags to keep the sea out.

Many people on the east coast felt that the Government response to the disaster was slow and inadequate but this certainly could not be said of voluntary organizations in the affected areas, and the local people themselves, who organized rescue and relief operations almost immediately. Mrs Nora Coles, a retired deputy headmistress from Skegness, described how, while living in lodgings at East Street, Alford, in Lincolnshire, she was woken at 1.00 a.m. on Sunday 1 February 1953 by her landlady. Mrs Coles was then senior mistress of Alford secondary modern school, and the headmaster, Mr B.C. Coles (later awarded the MBE for his services to the community during the disaster) was summoning the staff to turn the school into a reception centre for those in the Sutton and Trusthorpe area who had been made homeless by the disaster. Mrs Coles remembers her astonishment at the speed with which plans came together, and how quickly the school was transformed into a welcome shelter for the bedraggled refugees. She continues:

The main hall became the area where the sad, wet and cold victims gathered until details could be taken. A science master, J.R. Abbot, who had been a major in the army, took charge of this side of the operation with military precision, and he and a team of helpers began tracing relatives who lived away, and organized the search for those who were away from their homes at the time the sea came over. A.J. Benjamin, senior master of the school, was a resident of Sutton and he and his family were themselves homeless and had been rescued and brought into the school. He knew all manner of invaluable details, local children's birthday parties, the times of cinema shows etc., which helped all those who went out to do the rescue work. His own children were brought to the school some time after himself, having been collected from an upstairs window of the cinema. It was not long before local firms were helping us. I remember Cadbury's sending a mobile cafe which was parked up in the school yard, serving hot chocolate all day and all night for a week. Our own canteen staff were soon at their cookers and using up the reserve stocks to keep hot meals at the ready. This little band was headed by a very able cook, Miss M. Marsh, who was an Alford resident.

One must imagine the categories of people we were attempting to house: there were those who were ill and dying; those who were suffering mentally from the shock of the flood; children who had infectious diseases; the physically handicapped; pregnant women, some of whom were about to give birth, and the tramps who had been rescued from dykes and hedge-rows. We curtained off the main hall into three sections and palliasses – I can't remember where they came from – were placed on the floor, and in one section we had the babies born; in the third, unfortunately, one person died, and in the centre section we had shocked people and their pets – we even had a monkey! The staff room became the isolation room and the domestic science room became the communal wash and bath room. What tales to tell of bathing and cleaning up the rescued vagrants!

The headmaster was at the centre of operations, permanently engaged in answering the telephone and relaying messages to the staff. Thousands of people passed through the school and, for several months after the immediate disaster had passed, the hall was out of action, bedding and stores being kept there in case they should be needed again. Mrs Coles and Mr H. Higham, a mathematics teacher, spent a whole term interviewing people and issuing clothing and permits for household goods until, gradually, life returned to normal. Mrs Coles particularly remembers the kindness of the local people and the way in which they co-operated for the common good. She and many others, she recalled, went for days and nights without sleep, but morale was good and spirits remained high.

Some of the most detailed and vivid accounts came from people who were young children at the time of the disaster. One of these was Judith Tester, ten years old in January 1953, and a native of Sutton-on-Sea. On the 31st, she and her five-year-old sister, Susan, were at a birthday party at the home of her friend Jennifer Baker. The children had just finished their tea and had started to play games when a mother, Mrs Betty Green, arrived to take home the children from the Church Lane area as sea-water was coming through the streets. She had decided to take the children across the fields from Alford Road to the railway station, but returned shortly after, saying that the fields were flooded. In the mean time, Mrs Baker had telephoned Judith's father to ask him to come and meet his daughters, and the girls were just putting on their outdoor shoes when the floodwaters burst in through the front door. Everyone – a dozen children and five adults – rushed upstairs, and when the lights went out shortly after the children were put to bed, four in each bed. Miss Tester writes:

> Next morning I can remember seeing Mr Baker trying to reach food by stepping on one wooden chair and placing another in front of him. It was so cold and wet everywhere, and as the bedrooms had small fireplaces, the adults tried to light fires with what wood they could find. A neighbour, Richard Simons, helped by climbing over the roofs of sheds and outhouses to give Mr Baker some dry wood.
>
> To keep us amused during that long cold Sunday morning, the eldest of the children, Adrian Benjamin, tried to tell us stories. As we were at the house of the manager of a mineral water factory, there were empty lemonade bottles floating around in the water, and as a crate would fall over the bottles would float away in groups and Adrian made up stories about the 'puddle ducks' as he called them. We watched the planes flying round and Adrian decided that if we waved from the window with one hand first and then the other, the pilots would think that there were twenty-six children in the house and we would be rescued more quickly. This exercise kept us occupied for ages. (Needless to say Adrian later went to Oxford University!)

The house was a tall one on the outskirts of Sutton, giving a clear view along the Alford Road, and Miss Tester describes seeing the first convoy of army lorries driving into Sutton. The drivers could only guess the position of the roads by trees and telegraph-poles, and occasionally a lorry would fall into a dyke, the soldiers abandoning it and climbing into the vehicle behind. The men swam and waded through the water to the houses and when they came to the Bakers' home the big lounge window was opened, a soldier sat astride the window-sill and the children were passed through and carried on the shoulders of another soldier to one of the lorries. The children were taken to the Beach Hotel in Sutton, and she continues:

> All around me was devastation – sand, rubble, shop windows broken and people and lorries rushing everywhere. I can clearly remember seeing one lady, a Mrs Jordan, sitting in the window of the Gents' Outfitters feeding her new born baby. We were then transferred to a DUKW and taken to Hannah, where we were put on a bus, but I remember distinctly walking to the edge of the tide and looking back towards Sutton, where all was covered in sea water. There were dead chickens, blown-up pigs, dead animals of all sorts and

straw, feathers and branches of trees. Everywhere was cold, damp
and smelly.

The sisters were taken to the church hall at Alford, where their
names were recorded and they were given hot drinks. Confused
and anxious they sat down to wait for the arrival of their parents.

The previous evening, after receiving the telephone call from
Mrs Baker, their father set out to pick them up, but finding
sea-water running down the road returned to put on his wellington
boots. Before he could set out again, though, the floodwaters
rushed up the drive and in through the french windows and front
door. Soon the lights went out and all they could do was to retreat
upstairs and climb into bed to keep warm. At 2 a.m., they were
awakened by a neighbour from the bungalow opposite, asking if
he could bring his wife and family in; they had placed their two
children, baby and dog on the dining-room table, but they
themselves had been standing in the water until they could bear
the cold no longer. He made several trips, swimming across with
his wife and children before finally crossing with a very welcome
basket of food. When dawn came all that was visible from the
windows was dirty sea-water, over which flew several small planes,
probably taking photographs for the newspapers. It was not until
that afternoon that they were picked up by soldiers wading
through the floodwaters towing rubber dinghies and eventually
they arrived at the Corn Exchange at Alford, from where Mr
Tester set out on a tour of the rest centres, anxiously looking for
his daughters. Overjoyed when he finally found them at the church
hall, he returned with them to the Corn Exchange, where Judith,
safe with her parents again, watched the farmers coming in frozen
and exhausted after milking their cows and driving them to higher
ground, and police and rescue workers, blue with cold and drunk
from the tots of rum given them to keep out the cold.

On the Monday morning, Judith, Susan and their mother set out
for Tunbridge Wells to stay with relatives, going first to the rest
centre which Mrs Coles had helped set up at Alford secondary
modern school, where the headmaster gave them a form stating
that they were evacuees and allowed to travel free of charge. Even
so, on their arrival at Kings Cross, unkempt and bedraggled with
only the clothes in which they stood, the porter would not let them
off the station platform without tickets. Finally, in the station
master's office, Mrs Tester told her story. Judith continues:

He was wonderful. We were taken to the first class waiting room
and he sent out his secretary to the Grand Northern Hotel to fetch a

hot meal for us. As we had to wait until 3.00 p.m. to get the train to Tunbridge Wells he gave Sue and I money to go and feed the pigeons in Trafalgar Square and he bought us comics to read. He personally got us a taxi to go across London to catch the connecting train and he phoned my uncle at his place of work to let him know we were safe and well, and on our way ... My grandparents at Tunbridge Wells were wonderful and sent around loads of clothes as we had nothing but what we were wearing. Many of the dresses I wore had the name Jessica Tasker in them, and I have often wondered who she was, and would like to thank her and her parents for the kind thoughts and clothes she let us have that year.'

Several of the letters I received described events of great sadness, such as that from Mr S. David Briggs who was six years old at the time of the disaster, and lived at Skegness. His parents' friends, John and Carol Jordan, lived about eight miles to the north, almost on the beach, near the village of Huttoft. Mr Briggs writes:

I will always have long memories of the Jordans' house at Huttoft. It was hardly a house, just a wooden structure that provided a cosy home, and a shop that sold beach goods, that basked in a bright Lincolnshire sunshine that seems to have been lost in recent years. The house was actually built on the beach, which stretched to the sea some distance away. It was reached by a road that sloped between buckthorn and marram grass and, to my small viewpoint, seemed to go on for miles – the telephone wires humming in the hot sun – till it took a sudden turn, and went the other way, and there was the Jordan's house, in the middle of the sand, where my mother and I used to spend many Saturday mornings.

My mother had met Carol in the W.A.A.F. and was anxious to keep old friendships going. Her husband was a general 'keeper' of the beach and sold toys and buckets and spades – but to whom on that lonely stretch of coast I cannot think. All I knew was that such days at Huttoft were paradise, as I played with Susan Jordan and her younger brother Johnny, who was little more than a toddler, on that flat stretch of sand with the Jordans' house in the background – how quiet and peaceful it was!

Such a paradise came to an end one dark, February day when Susan stayed at our house, and my grandmother took her and myself to the Tower 'pullover' which stretched down to Skegness beach. There was little to see besides stretches of water that lay on the road, and wooden boxes and pieces of wood littering the seafront. I had no real conception of what had happened, except that it was something important, and that this silent visit to the seafront had something to do with it. Susan's mother was not with us, even though she had stayed at our house.

The real drama, of which we merely saw the ragged results, had happened the previous night. Mrs Jordan and Susan had spent the day with us at Skegness, Mr Jordan and young Johnny staying at home. As Susan and her mother were preparing to get the last bus home to Huttoft they were confronted at the door by my uncle, who asked where they were going.

'Back to Huttoft', was the reply.

'Oh no you're not', he retorted, 'you'll stay here. The road is cut off from the rest of the coast, north of Ingoldmells.' Later that same night, Huttoft, which in 1953 was just beach and sand-dunes, was submerged, and the Jordans lost their home. John Jordan survived but was unable to save his son, who was lost to the sea.

Shortly after, the Jordans emigrated to Australia where, when Mr Briggs last heard from them, they had settled down. They wrote without bitterness of the event, but Carol asked Mr Briggs to send her a few stones from the beach at Huttoft.

Norfolk

The greatest losses occurred on the Norfolk coast, amongst the bungalows situated on the low-lying land between King's Lynn and Hunstanton. The flimsily built bungalows were intended to be holiday homes but now they were permanently occupied, some by American servicemen and their families. Sixty-five people, including thirteen Americans, were killed in the bungalows which were torn from their foundations and tossed around like toys by the gigantic waves, one of them being thrown bodily across the Hunstanton-to-Lynn railway line. The 7.27 p.m. train had just left Hunstanton and, about halfway between there and Heacham was met by a gigantic wave, carrying the bungalow on its crest. The bungalow struck the engine on the smoke-box, damaging the vacuum-brake pipe and bringing it to a halt. The lights failed, the engine fire went out, debris battered the train and passengers had to stand on seats to keep out of the water. After six hours the engine-driver and his crew succeeded in making a temporary repair to the brake, and, using the floorboards of the tender as fuel, raised sufficient steam to propel the train slowly back to Hunstanton.

Mr A.G. James of Great Yarmouth wrote to me describing sad events of the floods along the Hunstanton–Heacham stretch of coast. In 1953 he was the headmaster of Hunstanton County primary school, the 350 pupils ranging from five to fifteen years old and including at least a dozen American children whose fathers were stationed at Sculthorpe Air Force base. Four of his pupils died in the floods, plus a girl of fifteen who had left his school that

Christmas and an American boy about to start at the school. Among the dead were fourteen-year-old Derek Stubbins and his sister Marjorie, aged nine, whose body Mr James had the sad task of identifying on the Sunday morning. The children's father was also lost, but their two elder sisters survived (the mother had previously left the family). Also killed were Jennifer Papworth, ten years old, and her sisters Susan aged eight and Patricia, fifteen. The American boy was Herbert Branch, aged six, whose father, mother and younger sister also drowned. Mr James concluded on a happier note:

> An American family named Buster with four children owed their lives to the initiative of the father. As their home began to flood, he got his wife and youngsters – the oldest, Ralph, just six a fortnight before – on top of the porch and, subsequently on to the roof. He went back below and brought up blankets and whiskey and, later, when he realized that the chimney stack was likely to fall, moved his family to the other side of it. They were eventually rescued after nine hours. The houses, mainly bungalows in the affected areas, were flimsily built, intended to be holiday homes, but due to the post-war housing shortage and the influx into the town of American services personnel, were now in all-year-round occupation. Their posts and wire garden fences proved severe obstacles to the amphibious vehicles brought in, such as the DUKWS. ... One very tall American serviceman [mentioned by several of my correspondents] waded for hours to homes to carry people out and was given a British decoration.

The tall American serviceman was USAF Corporal Reis Leming, from Sculthorpe, who was the first non-British recipient of the George Medal. Twenty-two years old, and a non-swimmer, he single-handedly rescued twenty-seven people from the South Beach area of Hunstanton. He waded in the icy waters for hours before collapsing from exposure. The efforts of the Americans generally in the rescue operations were warmly praised by many people living in East Anglia.

Strangely, a few weeks after I received Mr James's letter, I heard from Mrs Elsie Plumb of Hunstanton, who, it transpired, was the aunt of the Papworth girls mentioned by Mr James. Mrs Plumb's sister, Phyllis Papworth, had, with her four daughters, occupied a bungalow at the bottom of Southbeach Road. At about six o'clock on that Saturday evening, Mrs Plumb's husband went out for a drink, only to dash back a few minutes later, saying that the sea had come in over Southbeach Road. Mrs Plumb at this stage did not realize the scale of disaster, but her husband went out again, returning about an hour later to describe the scenes of devastation and the efforts being made by the Americans – among whom was a corporal, Reis Leming – to get the people out. Mrs Plumb now grasped the seriousness of the situation and became very anxious about her sister in Southbeach Road. With a six-month-old baby, she could do nothing that night, but on the Sunday morning she learned that many people had been drowned, and, the mortuary being full, the dead were being taken to the town hall. She knew that Janet Papworth had been at a birthday party at the house of her friends the Turners and hurried down to see her, but the twelve-year-old girl knew little of the disaster. Mrs Plumb then made her way to Southbeach Road, the lower end of which was the scene of absolute confusion. She could see her sister's bungalow, but it had been shifted by the force of the floods, and Mrs Plumb suddenly realized that it had been turned completely round, back to front. She took off her shoes and began to walk down the road, but an American officer stopped her, saying that all the people had been taken out. She then rushed frantically back to town, to the Sandringham Hotel where the names of the dead had been written on a large board, but the Papworths' names were not listed. Mrs Plumb then went to the town hall but again there was no news of her relatives, so she began to think they might be safe. On the Monday, however, a friend of the Plumbs, walking along Southbeach Road, looked through the broken windows of the Papworths' bungalow and to his horror saw Phyllis and three of her daughters lying dead and covered with mud. He rushed to the Plumbs' house but could not even speak. Mrs Plumb guessed immediately what had happened. Their dog, Trixie, had managed to escape and, exhausted and with several ribs broken, had found her way to the Turners' house, throwing herself at Janet's feet. The twelve-year-old girl then also knew that her family had gone for ever.

Janet Papworth was looked after by the social services at Norwich for a while, then married an American at the age of seventeen and moved to the United States, where she died at the age of forty. The names of Phyllis Papworth and her three daughters are among those listed on a plaque in the public gardens at Hunstanton.

A dramatic, but happier, account concerning events in the Heacham area came from Mrs Sylvia Smith, now living at Clacton-on-Sea in Essex. In 1953 she and her three children,

Frank aged fourteen, Rosemary, twelve and Warren, eight, were living in a bungalow, 'Briarwood', also in Southbeach Road, about three-quarters-of-a-mile from the sea. They had just finished their tea on that Saturday afternoon when Rosemary, who had taken the dishes into the kitchen, called to her mother that water was coming under the back door. Mrs Smith went to investigate and found that it was sea-water, forcing its way in with frightening rapidity. The family went up on to the verandah, but the water still rose, so they decided to climb on to the roof. The two youngest children were helped up first, then Frank told his mother to climb up. As Mrs Smith started to scramble up, though, the entire verandah suddenly came away from the house, throwing her into the icy, swirling waters. Mrs Smith couldn't swim, and would almost certainly have drowned had not Frank swum out to her and hauled her back to the bungalow. The shivering pair managed to get on to the roof, and then crouched with the rest of the family near the chimney, continually shouting for help. It was a pitch-black night, bitterly cold, and without a sound to indicate the presence of other human beings. It seemed, recalled Mrs Smith, as if the world had come to an end. The Smiths stayed on the roof for some six hours, freezing cold, and watched the water as it rose higher and higher, almost covering the apple tree which stood in the garden, and starting, alarmingly, to lap against the roof of the bungalow. At last, however, the tide turned and the water stopped rising. At about midnight the Smiths saw lights and people who fetched a boat to their rescue. Mrs Smith continues:

> When they came with the boat we each in turn slid down the roof, and I heard screams each time one of the children went down. When it was my turn I found out why: they were unable to get the boat near enough so had tied it to the bungalow with a piece of rope and left a floating plank for us to land on. Of course, as each of us landed on it, it went under and we were again immersed in the sea. They got us all off but the rope went round my neck and I was nearly strangled!

The Smiths were taken to the village school where there was a roaring fire and warm beds ready for them, the staff, Mrs Smith recalled, looking after them with great kindness. The next day her husband arrived – he had been in Clacton to where the family were due to move the following week – and he went to the bungalow to salvage what he could. Mrs Smith was delighted when he found her engagement ring by feeling with his hands in the mud behind the dressing-table, and amazed that such a small object should have been retrieved when so many larger items had been washed away. Shortly after their removal to Clacton, the Smiths saw on a newsreel at the cinema Reis Leming being awarded the George Medal – he had been among the rescue party which had saved the Smiths and so many others that night.

Suffolk
Mrs J. Mitchell was living in Wilders Street in the Beach Village area of Lowestoft with her mother at the time of the disaster, her husband, who was in the RAF, spending a weekend's leave with them. That evening a policeman knocked at the cottage door to inform them that waves were coming over the sea-wall and that flooding was imminent. Even as he spoke, floodwater was nearing the house, and there was just time for Mr Mitchell to put two armchairs on the table before it burst in. Mrs Mitchell continues:

> We made our way upstairs, thinking that it wouldn't be much but when it reached the fifth stair I started to panic. My husband started going down the stairs to see what he could do, but at this point there was an almighty bang and a blue flash as the electric meter blew up. Along the road from our house was a large area containing enormous tree trunks which were stacked up high and these now began to float rapidly down the street. Several struck our house, which was right on the corner, with such force that the building shook.
>
> By midnight small boats appeared, rescuing people, but because our row of cottages was in a hollow they couldn't get to us, and we were marooned until the next morning. Even then the water was still four feet deep and my husband had to piggy-back me out ... The next day was absolutely heartbreaking: as the water receded it left a stinking mass of mud and sludge. The large wooden table my mother had in the front room had a drawer containing all the family photos etc. and these were ruined. It was a terrifying ordeal – not being able to escape and not knowing how much further the water would rise.

Mrs Dorrie Green was living on a ten acre smallholding, close to the River Deben, some five miles inland from Felixstowe, with her husband and three sons, thirteen, ten and five years old. The house was large and detached and faced the sea. On the night of the flood Mrs Green was recovering in bed from flu, and it was only in the morning when her husband got up and drew back the curtains that they realized what had happened. 'My God!', he exclaimed, 'We're surrounded – flooded!' Mrs Green staggered out of bed and across to the window where all she could see was a continuous sheet of water stretching from their house to the sea. The Greens dressed hurriedly, checked on their livestock and greenhouses – where the anthracite cinders in the heaters were sizzling in the floodwaters – and then drove to Felixstowe where their thirteen-year-old son was at school. While they were there they heard reports that many people in prefabs in the Langer Road area had been drowned, but details at that time were lacking. Mrs Green writes:

> On our return home my husband and thirteen-year-old son rowed about rescuing hens and piglets, which had been stranded, in our rowing boat. The local authority organised men to fill in the breaks in the River Deben wall which had been made by the wind-driven tide. They dropped hundreds of bags of cement into the hole, but it was no use, the hole was so big. In the end they brought a gigantic iron girder from the north of England to drop into the gap, and I remember the traffic problems it caused as they tried to manoeuvre it along the roads. Anyway, late that night my husband arrived home after working at the wall, covered in white cement dust with a bright red face – he too had caught the flu and was running a high temperature so I put him to bed. Then my son went down with it too, so I had to nurse them, look after the other two children, run the smallholding, look after 3,000 hens and stoke the boilers.
>
> Later that month we were driving to Ipswich and stopped to give a lift to a woman. She was very strange and we soon learned the reason why, as she poured out her 'flood story'. She had lived with her husband in a prefab in Langer Road and awakened to hear water gurgling. Climbing out of bed she stepped into water, and immediately woke her husband and shouted to him to follow her out of the window. He either wouldn't or couldn't, and he drowned. The woman spent half the night on the roof in her nightdress, and was rescued in the morning, frozen almost to death. The experience had left the poor woman quite deranged.

The worst hit area of Suffolk was indeed the Langer Road area of Felixstowe, where there was an estate of post-war prefabricated bungalows. The bungalows caught the full force of the inundation, and each one was torn from its foundations, some ending up two hundred yards away. Charles Durrant of Langer Road was awakened by the sound of the floodwater and looking out could only see a sheet of water. The Durrants had only time to put on their dressing-gowns and rouse their children before water started coming up through the floor. Mr Durrant, his wife who was pregnant, and two children managed to scramble up on to the porch, and then on to the roof, where they spent a miserable five hours, freezing cold and wet through, before they were rescued. 'I didn't know what to think', Mr Durrant later commented. 'Everything was so quiet, with the moon shining down. I wondered if the end of the world had come.' In the taller houses on the opposite side of Langer Road people were awakened by the screams of prefab residents as they tried to climb on to their roofs. The Hillary family who occupied a flat overlooking the estate watched in horror as the bungalows were swept away. 'As one floated past we saw a woman washed off it', said Mrs Hillary. At least thirty-nine people were drowned at Langer Road, and on the following Tuesday morning their relatives had the harrowing task of identifying the bodies in Felixstowe town hall.

Many flood survivors, trapped on roofs or the upper floors of their houses, mentioned the eerie effect of darkness and lack of any sound of human activity. Mrs Annette Parker, for example, who lived in a flat over a café near Cavendish Road in Felixstowe commented:

> As the evening wore on, the sea started to come up over the promenade and I went downstairs to the road to see what was happening and actually saw the sea starting to come down the road. I went upstairs and looking out saw the road was like a river. Myself

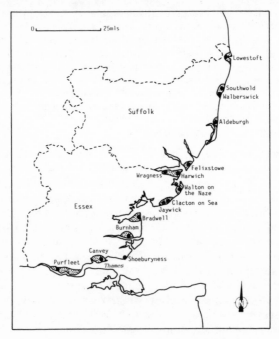

Fig.13. Areas of Suffolk and Essex affected by the floods of 1953

A souvenir of the 1739 frost fair, printed on the ice

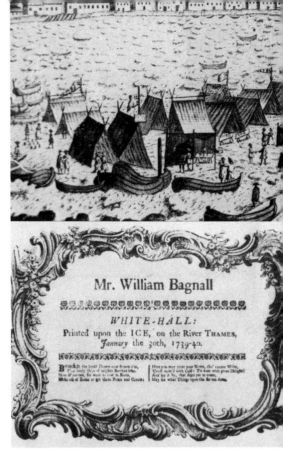

Mr. William Bagnall

WHITE-HALL:
Printed upon the ICE, on the River THAMES,
January the 30th, 1739-40.

BEHOLD the liquid Thames now frozen o'er, | Here you may print your Name, tho' cannot Write,
That lately Ships of mighty Burthen bore. | 'Cause none so weak Call't: Tis done with great Delight!
Now Wherries, for want to row in Boats, | And lay it by, that ages yet to come,
Whole rick of House to get them Pence and Groats: | May see what Things upon the Ice was done.

Frost fair on the Thames in 1814

A remarkable early photograph of wrecked locomotives at the
New Cross engine-shed which collapsed during a gale in 1863

Wreckage of the Tay Bridge destroyed in the severe gale of
28 December 1879

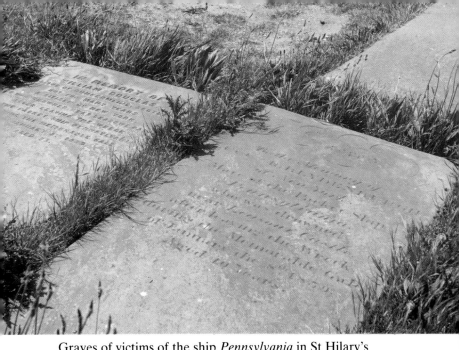

Graves of victims of the ship *Pennsylvania* in St Hilary's churchyard, Wallasey

The north-east slope of Meldon Hill, showing the exposed peat base after a bog-slide in heavy rain in July 1963

Fish fall in east London. Ronald Langton shows two of the
flounders which fell into his yard in June 1984

and other people in flats in the large houses were all very scared – we thought the world was coming to an end.

Essex

Canvey Island, like the Heacham area of Norfolk, consisted largely of a sprawling, unplanned mass of shacks and bungalows. It was a popular location for holiday homes but, again as at Heacham, many of these were now occupied all the year round. Many of Canvey's residents were elderly, having retired to homes by the sea after a lifetime's work in London, and they were ill-equipped to deal with the floods. The island was the scene of the largest evacuation of the east coast disaster: within forty-eight hours its entire population was taken off, with the exception of fifty-eight of the inhabitants for whom rescue tragically came too late.

A few of Canvey's inhabitants seem to have had just time enough to get up into attics or roof spaces before the floodwaters struck, but most were still in their beds when, with a tremendous roar, the sea-wall was breached and the water burst through upon their homes. Many of the victims died there and then in bed, others suffered a slow death – standing for hours up to their necks in water, or slipping into the floodwaters exhausted after desperately clinging to roofs or floating wreckage. Some died days, even weeks, afterwards, from the effects of shock and exposure. There were some remarkable escapes, however: Charles Stevens was awakened by the barking of his dog and getting out of bed found his feet were in water. Minutes later the bungalow was flooded but he had managed to scramble on to the top of the wardrobe and punch a hole in the plasterboard ceiling, pulling his wife and children up into the roof space. They spent eleven hours in the dark and cold, soaking wet and listening to the screams of people around them, before they were rescued, but as Mr Stevens commented, 'If it hadn't been for the dog we would have drowned as we slept.' Not so fortunate were Mr Stevens's daughter and son-in-law who lived across the road. Trapped in their house they seemed to have spent the last few minutes of their lives trying to float their baby, Linda, to safety in a pram. Mercifully the child was later pulled alive out of the wreckage by a rescue worker.

It was a grim, tragic task, methodically searching the flooded island for the dead and missing, with frantic relatives trying to push past soldiers and police to go looking for themselves. With horrible regularity the boats would come down the flooded streets, carrying bodies wrapped in blankets. A fireman, Mickey Sanders, later commented:

The worst thing was finding the bodies of people you had known all your life. We had to lay about eighteen or twenty bodies out on the pavement to be identified. They were all people I actually knew. You can't imagine what it was like.

A further thirty-seven people were drowned at Jaywick, which, like Canvey Island, was a settlement of mostly retired people, living in bungalows and chalets, the average age of those killed being sixty-five. As at Canvey Island, some survived by climbing into their attics, one elderly woman surviving for thirty-one hours in her roof space, with her cat, after her chalet was overturned. Mrs P.K. Carr of Whetstone in London was just about to move to a chalet in Fern Way, Jaywick, at the time of the floods, having signed the contract two days before. She recalls:

I remember coming down soon afterwards. I had to get on to a lorry at the beginning of Golf Green Road to get through. My chalet was still unmoved and the water had gone down somewhat, but it had left a mark five feet high on the walls. The next door chalet, though, was uprooted and standing on my fence.

At Harwich, further up the Essex coast, the pier was submerged and the quay, the esplanade and the Bathside area to the west were flooded. One account which captures graphically the fear, confusion and tragedy is that from Mrs Yvonne Roberts of Dovercourt in Essex who in 1953 was fourteen years old, and living with her parents, three sisters and brother in Albert Street, Harwich, the house having six rooms, two below ground level comprising a small basement. The family were all asleep, but Yvonne was awakened by the wind and, looking out of the window, saw water running down the steps into the basement. She woke her sisters, Edna and Ivy, and they all stood at the window, frightened and uncertain what to do, when they heard a neighbour, Harry Rodger, shouting up to her parents from the street that there was a flood. When he saw their lights come on he ran back down the street, pursued by the water which was soon up to his waist. The family formed a human chain on the stairs to try to save some of their possessions, which included the eldest sister's wedding dress, hanging on the back of the living-room door. The dress was saved, along with several wedding presents, and Yvonne's father, thinking that the flood was only going to be a few inches, stood the chairs on the kitchen table. Suddenly, though, there was a great thud on the front door and an enormous wall of water burst into the room. Mrs Roberts continues: 'Mum grabbed at Dad but missed him, then my sister grabbed him and she and Mum got Dad upstairs. We then started to hurriedly get my sister's clothes and wedding presents up the second flight of stairs, then collected up what we could from Mum and Dad's bedroom.'

The family, cold and miserable, waited for morning to come. Yvonne's father was looking out for a long time, watching for the wall opposite to reappear above the water, indicating that the level had dropped, but then suddenly realized that the wall itself had been washed away! When it eventually grew light the family opened the window and called to their neighbours who were also trapped in their upstairs rooms. Mrs Roberts recalls drinking the water from their hot-water bottles, and her mother's anger when the police shouted up to turn their gas and electricity off – the stop-cocks were under fifteen to twenty feet of water! Eventually they saw boats coming towards them, crewed with young men from the training ship *Ganges* at Shotley, and they were soon rescued. Ivy, Edna, Peter and Yvonne were taken off first, the latter shocked at the great amount of debris – dead cats, pigs, doors and mattresses – that was floating past, the boat then returning for their parents and oldest sister, Sylvia. As the children were being rowed down the street they were frightened to see the body of a local man hanging out of a window where he had been trying to rescue Mrs Bruce and her new-born son, both of whom perished. The children were taken to the Anchor pub in the High Street, where they were transferred to army lorries and driven to a drill hall to be given food and drinks. They were still clad only in their nightclothes with coats on top, and had a long and miserable wait before their parents and sister were brought to them, the last to be rescued from Albert Street. The family was then taken to a transit camp where they stayed for several months; Yvonne, however, was one of ten children whose names were drawn to go on a month's trip to Germany. Mrs Roberts concludes: 'I hope this gives some idea of what happened that terrible night. I know I will never forget it.'

This chapter has been concerned with the initial impact of the east coast floods. Little has been written of the long term effects – the tremendous efforts needed to repair the sea defences, houses, roads and communications; and the attempts of thousands of people to clean and dry their homes, and try to rebuild their shattered lives. For many families, of course, life never could be the same again, for they had lost not just their homes, but their sons, daughters, parents, friends and relatives. The plight of many of the evacuated families was in one respect worse than that of the wartime evacuees, who had at least had time to pack suitcases: many of the flood victims were evacuated with nothing but the clothes – often nightclothes – they were wearing at the time. Hilda Grieve, who wrote an exhaustive study of the effect of the flood on the county of Essex asserted: 'The sea's achievement in one night challenges comparison with that of the *Luftwaffe* in six years.'

6 Great Gales

Tragedy in Liverpool Bay

The great gale of 1839 has not received the same attention as that of 1703, but it would seem to have been hardly less ferocious. At least 185 people were killed; thousands of trees were blown down; hundreds of buildings were destroyed or badly damaged and many ships were wrecked, though there was not the huge loss of life at sea which occurred in 1703. It was mainly the south of England that suffered in 1703, but in 1839 the fury of the storm was concentrated on north-west England, north Wales, Scotland and Ireland. The year had begun with a spell of fine weather, but late on the afternoon of Sunday 6 January, there was a change; the barometer fell sharply and by midnight the wind had reached hurricane force, its strength being such that salt spray from the Irish Sea was carried many miles inland, as far east, amazingly, as Alford in Lincolnshire (130 miles) according to the Boston newspaper, *Star in the East*. It is hard to single out any particularly tragic episode in a night which witnessed many tragedies, but perhaps the greatest disaster was the wrecking of the ships *Brighton, Lockwoods, St Andrew* and *Pennsylvania* in Liverpool Bay.

The gale seems to have been at its worst during the early hours of Monday morning, 7 January, but it continued to rage throughout Monday and Tuesday. There was great anxiety in Liverpool concerning the ships which had left the port on the high tide (about 3 p.m.) on Sunday, but nothing was known of their fate until Tuesday, when several, battered by the storm, arrived back in the Mersey. Some went ashore at Bootle, in the estuary, where, owing to the shelving nature of the beaches, there seems to have been little, if any, loss of life, while other vessels managed to reach safe anchorages. One of these was HM steamship *Meteor* which was bound from Liverpool to Portsmouth with twenty-two prisoners for transportation to Van Diemen's Land, now Tasmania. The ship was thrown around mercilessly by the storm in the Irish Sea, and the crew had given up hope, but the master finally managed to put back to port, anchoring in the Bight of Sloyne, on the Birkenhead side of the Mersey at 2.30 on Tuesday afternoon. On their way in, they reported they had passed several wrecks, including the *Brighton*, the *Lockwoods*, the *St Andrew* and the *Pennsylvania*. The *Brighton* had apparently grounded late on Monday, and early Tuesday morning, Mr James Atherton of New Brighton, a wealthy Liverpool merchant, had summoned one of the Liverpool–Seacombe steam ferry-boats to go to her assistance. The Magazines (New Brighton) lifeboat also went out and the two boats rescued the captain and those of the crew still on board; fourteen seamen had taken to a raft after the ship had grounded but they seem to have perished, for nothing more was heard of them.

The *Lockwoods*, *St Andrew* and *Pennsylvania* had sailed from Liverpool on Sunday's high tide, all three being first-class packet-ships bound for New York with valuable cargoes and emigrants excited at the prospect of new lives in America. Henry Aspinall, a young lad from Birkenhead who watched the ships' departure, later recalled: 'Flags were flying, and the passengers full of bright anticipation for the future. Many of the emigrants came from the continent, though natives of the British Isles predominated. Within thirty-six hours most of these poor people were drowned, almost within speaking distance of land.'

The three ships had reached as far west as Holyhead when, in the early hours of Monday morning, the wind changed, veering from WSW to NW and soon reached gale force. One of the passengers on board the *Pennsylvania*, Henry Graham Thompson of New York, later reported:

> It blew a complete hurricane, and soon carried away all our sails, and many of our spars. I was seasick, and being below part of the night did not see all that occurred. The storm continued throughout Monday, and we did not know where we were, the spray was so thick. We were, in fact, drifting at the mercy of the wind and waves.

It was impossible to run up any more sails, as no man could even keep his feet on deck. All day the *Pennsylvania* was tossed around by the moutainous seas, and during the Monday night everyone on board thought she would break up. She held together, though, and on Tuesday morning her crew realized that they were off the Ormes Head on the north Wales coast. They managed to hoist some sails and set course for Liverpool.

The *Lockwoods* had undergone a similar ordeal, as her first mate, Thomas Fleck described:

> The last land we saw was between Point Lynas and the Great Ormes Head. The next morning we could not tell exactly where we were, as we had been drifting down the Lancaster [*sic*] coast. We then wore the ship round, and made for Liverpool. After leaving Black Combe, the next land we made was about the Ormes Head, the gale still blowing. It was then about ten o'clock on Tuesday. As we had no canvas to take the ship out, we bore towards Liverpool. We kept the lead constantly going, and by means of that and the run we had made, we expected to have seen the floating light about twelve o'clock, or else a pilot boat ... Not seeing the lightship to guide us we were all abroad in our calculations.

The absence of the lightship, and the confusion this caused, was later stressed by several passengers and crew members, Edmund Tompkins, one of the *Lockwoods'* crew, asserting that had the lightship been visible all would have been safe. By about midday on Tuesday the three ships had reached the mouth of the Mersey (Tompkins stated that his ship had got as far as the Spencer Gut Buoy). At this stage everyone on board the three ships was safe, but now, almost within hailing distance of land, disaster struck. The ships dropped anchor, hoping to ride out the gale, but the wind was too strong, the chains snapped, and the vessels were driven on to the sandbanks off Leasowe, on the north coast of the Wirral, to be relentlessly pounded by the waves.

At about three o'clock that afternoon, Henry Thompson, the passenger on the *Pennsylvania* mentioned earlier, managed to get off the ship in the jollyboat with the first and second mate, five crew members and at least three passengers. It was hopeless attempting to row – all the men could do was to try to keep the boat heading towards the shore. Despite the howling gale and enormous waves they managed to get to within a mile of land when the boat was swamped and Thompson thrown into the sea. A wave broke over him and the next thing he saw was the upturned boat with three or four of its occupants clinging to the keel. Two others, Mr Parsons and Mr Suitor were in the water. On shore, meanwhile, anxious watchers saw the boat capsize and then watched as several of the men attempted to swim ashore. As they drew closer, those on shore waded out into the sea and formed a human chain in a desperate attempt to rescue them. They succeeded in bringing Henry Thompson ashore still alive, but the others, frozen and exhausted, were drowned. The bodies of Lucas

T. Blydenburgh, mate of the *Pennsylvania*, and Mr Parsons, one
of the passengers, were recovered and taken to the Leasowe
Castle Hotel. Also taken to the hotel were William Douglas,
another passenger, who was picked up further along the coast by
the keeper of the Leasowe lighthouse. Mr Douglas was still alive
when picked up, but died shortly after, at the hotel, despite all
efforts to revive him.

Meanwhile, tragedy had struck on the *Pennsylvania* herself.
Shortly after the jollyboat had been launched an attempt was made
to launch the longboat, but a huge sea broke over the ship,
smashing the longboat and causing Captain Smith to try to jump
into the rigging. He fell, however, and before he could regain his
feet was washed overboard by another huge wave. The third mate,
Mr Richard, then ordered those left on board to climb into the
rigging and followed them himself.

At the very time these tragic events were taking place, ships
were on their way to the rescue. At about midday, the steamer
Mountaineer had tried to approach the *St Andrew*, fast on the
sandbank, but the gale was still too fierce to attempt a rescue, so
she went to the assistance of another vessel, the *Ward*, which only
needed an anchor and cable, and then to a sloop, ashore on the
West Hoyle Bank. This vessel was deserted and the *Mountaineer*
then proceeded to the *Lockwoods* and *Pennsylvania* and waited
for the wind to abate.

Meawhile, a steam-tug, the *Victoria*, under the command of
Captain Eccles, had left Liverpool pierhead at 1.30 p.m. Tuesday,
and stopped to pick up the Magazines (New Brighton) lifeboat, a
sailing/rowing craft, which she towed out to the *St Andrew*, coming
abreast of her at about 3.30. The lifeboat and the *Victoria*'s own
boat went across to the stricken ship and succeeded in rescuing
twenty-three people, and while the *Mountaineer* stood by to pick
up those remaining on the *St Andrew*, the *Victoria* set out towards
the other wrecks, towing the New Brighton lifeboat. Now,
however, an unhappy disagreement marred the splendid rescue
attempt: the crew of the lifeboat (which was heavily laden with
survivors from the *St Andrew*) insisted upon returning to shore, for
which they were later to be severely criticized.

The captain of the *Lockwoods* with five of the crew, who had
taken to a gig in an attempt to get help for their vessel, were
picked up and transferred to the steam-tug *Victoria* by a pilot boat
which had arrived on the scene. The *Lockwoods*' captain begged
Captain Eccles to try to save those left on his ship, and the
steam-tug went in under *Lockwoods*' stern repeatedly, and at

enormous risk to herself, and took off twenty-six persons, until, with the tide now dangerously low and night approaching, Captain Eccles was forced to return to shore.

Fifty-six people had so far been saved from the wrecks, but a terrible ordeal lay ahead for those left on board the vessels. The weather that night was atrocious with snow and a biting wind, and three members of the *Pennsylvania*'s crew perished in the rigging. The situation on the *Lockwoods* was even worse, as Thomas Fleck, first mate, later described:

> It was about three o'clock on the morning of Wednesday that the ship began to break up, part of the passengers were in the mizzen rigging and part in the mizzen top; but fearing the masts would fall, we all came down again to the poop. The sea was at this time washing right over us, and there were only two of the crew besides myself left on board, all the rest, excepting one who was drowned during the night, having been taken away by the *Victoria*. From the time the steam-tug left us on Tuesday night, till the following morning, a great number of the passengers perished. I counted about thirty dead on the poop in the morning, all of whom, I think died from the cold and the sea washing over them.

Captain Eccles wasted no time in renewing his heroic rescue work. By 4 a.m. on Wednesday morning, having taken on fresh coals, extra crew and towing two gigs, the *Victoria* was on her way again, and by 7 a.m. was abreast of the wrecks. The fury of the storm prevented the two open gigs from going across, but the arrival of a fishing boat from Hoylake helped the rescue work to continue; this boat made two trips to the *Lockwoods* and brought twenty-two people safely to the tug. In Captain Eccles's words:

> During this time, despatched one of our gigs to the *Pennsylvania*, which brought off a part of her crew to us; and the Magazines life-boat, which had come up, also made two trips, and brought from that vessel a number of others. At this time, the lifeboat from Hoylake came to us; desired them to go to the *Lockwoods*, to bring off a man and his wife, the woman being in a helpless state, her husband being unwilling to leave her, and unable to assist her into the fishing boat; after which proceeded to Liverpool with the persons saved – twenty-two from the *Lockwoods*, and twenty-six from the *Pennsylvania*; making a total, saved by the *Victoria* tug, of one hundred and four persons.

Captain Eccles, to whose bravery and skill so many owed their lives, shared the opinion that had the New Brighton lifeboat not returned to shore on that first day everyone on board the

Lockwoods and the *Pennsylvania* could have been saved: twenty-seven died on the *Lockwoods* and fourteen on the *Pennsylvania*.

The inquests were held at the Leasowe Castle Hotel at the end of the week. In a stable lay the bodies of Edward Parsons and Mr Suitor, passengers on the *Pennsylvania*, and Lucas Blydenburgh, her first mate, the body of William Douglas, another *Pennsylvania* passenger lying in a room inside the hotel. Statements from passengers and members of the crew were heard, and Peter Roberts, an Irishman who lived in Hoylake, described how he and several others had gone out to the wreck of the *Lockwoods* on Thursday morning and found twenty-one bodies – men, women and children – in various positions on the poop deck. Two more bodies were discovered on the main deck and with the others were taken to a workhouse in Liverpool. The bodies of a woman and a boy were in the rigging, but were so tightly entangled, said Roberts, that he could not get them free. Later, however, Joshua Howell of Liverpool, Clerk to the Commissioner of Police, succeeded in removing them and they were also taken to Liverpool.

Criticism was levelled at the captain of the *Lockwoods* for leaving his ship, but there were several witnesses who spoke up in his defence: it was said that he had done all in his power to assist as the *Victoria* snatched survivors from his vessel, and that he was on board the *Victoria* when she set out again the next day.

Verdicts of 'Accidental Drowning' were recorded: the efforts of those involved in the rescue operations, particularly Captain Eccles, were highly praised, while the conduct of the crew of the New Brighton lifeboat was criticized. A report subsequently called for by the Dock Committee paid tribute to the crew for the lives they had saved but also concluded on a note of censure:

> Considering the services which the crew of the Magazines Lifeboat accurately performed in saving the lives of some of the crew and passengers, numbering 47 persons, from the ships wrecked in the recent gales, and notwithstanding this, the Committee still regrets their casting-off from the steam-tug at the time they did.

The story of the Liverpool Bay tragedy is based on contemporary reports, mainly from the *Liverpool Mercury*, the forerunner of the *Liverpool Echo*, and there is no doubt that there was much public resentment voiced against the Magazines lifeboat crew at the time. Later, it seems, there were some who thought perhaps it was unfair: after all, the crew had been in disagreement with Captain

Eccles, a strong character, regarded, rightly, as a hero, and it is likely that his views would prevail.

Not surprisingly, the shattered hulks of the packet-ships acted as a magnet to looters and scavengers, of whom hundreds descended on to the Wirral shores to plunder the goods washed up. The Chief Constable of Liverpool sent over a large contingent of police, armed with cutlasses, to deal with them: there were skirmishes and numerous arrests, and many small boats which went out to the wrecks as the gale subsided were seized by the port police as they re-entered the Mersey laden with plunder of every description.

William Douglas and Lucas T. Blydenburgh were buried close to the old tower of St Hilary's Church in Wallasey. Standing today by their time-weathered gravestones, one can look across the Wirral fields to the Leasowe Castle Hotel, where their bodies were taken, and beyond to the sandbanks on which their ship was wrecked, over a century and a half ago.

The Tay Bridge Disaster

The achievements of the Victorian engineers transformed the landscape and society of nineteenth-century Britain, some of their most impressive and elegant creations being the great bridges such as those at Menai, Saltash and Clifton. The railway bridge over the River Tay at Dundee seemed a natural successor to the works of Telford and Brunel, and was widely regarded as one of the greatest structural achievements of the age, being, at two miles, the longest bridge in the world. Engineering and technology, it seemed, could surmount all difficulties, and smooth the way for ever-expanding industry. However, the nation's confidence suffered a tremendous blow on 28 December 1879 when, at the height of an exceptionally severe gale, the Tay Bridge was blown down, carrying with it a train and killing seventy-five people.

The Tay Bridge, designed by Thomas Bouch, was officially opened on 1 June 1878, having been seven years in construction. It consisted of a superstructure of latticed iron girders, supported by eighty-five piers, and carried a single track railway line across the firth. The middle section of the bridge was 3,185 feet long and consisted of thirteen sections, each 245 feet in length; it was eighty-eight feet above the surface of the water, the girders rearing upwards for a further twenty-seven feet. On this middle section the railway track was carried by the lower edges of the latticework, while on the shore sections the track was supported by the upper edges of the lattice. The bridge was originally to have been supported by brick piers, but it was discovered that the river-bed, instead of consisting of hard sandstone, was composed of sandy clay and gravel, and that consequently some of the piers would have to be lighter. The final design for the middle section, therefore, included masonry bases, the tops of which protruded some five feet above high water, surmounted by cast-iron columns. These iron pillars were eighty-three feet high, there being six of them to each pier. Each was cast in seven lengths, bolted together through flanges at their ends. The pillars of each pier were held together with wrought-iron stays. The structure was widely regarded as a triumph of the latest engineering practice, one contemporary account recording that, 'The bridge over the River Tay was believed to be the very perfection of strength as well as beauty.'

Albert Grothe, the Dutch engineer who superintended the building operations, was extremely proud of the bridge, perhaps tempting providence by his assertion that its strength would be sufficient to withstand the greatest gale that could sweep down the Tay. His enthusiasm spread among the local people: VIPs were invited to inspect the building operations, and in a fever of pride all manner of sweets, foods and articles were manufactured in its honour, including 'Tay Bridge Sauce' and 'Tay Bridge Toffee': a new era seemed to dawn upon Dundee. Numerous branch railway lines were built, linking the bridge with outlying areas, and thousands of working people crossed the bridge on Saturday afternoons to enjoy the scenery and fresh air of the Fife Hills. The ultimate seal of approval came during the summer of 1879 when Queen Victoria, *en route* from Balmoral to the south, visited Dundee with her entourage and crossed the bridge. On 26 June, Thomas Bouch went to Windsor to receive his knighthood.

Despite the air of general optimism, however, there were unhappy omens. No fewer than twenty men lost their lives in accidents during construction. There were continual financial difficulties and during a gale on 2 February 1877, two gigantic girders, which had not yet been secured, were blown into the river together with masonry and timber. Almost miraculously no one was killed, but the accident caused considerable delay and extra expense, and foreshadowed the tragedy to come. As is often the case with pioneering achievements there were numerous gloomy prognostications: the bridge was too narrow; it was too high; the middle section was top-heavy, etc. Dire warnings came from one Patrick Matthew, apparently a clairvoyant known as the Seer of Gourdie, who listed all manner of improbable disasters which could befall the bridge, including destruction by earthquake and ramming by a ship manned by drunken sailors, but one of his warnings echoed the fears of many local people: quite simply the bridge would not be strong enough to withstand the gales that swept down the Tay. Afterwards, the *Newcastle Chronicle* commented: 'Mr Matthew has been gathered to his fathers, but had he lived until the night of Sunday, 28th December, 1879, and seen the broken bridge, and the crowds that lined the river at Dundee, he must have had a gloomy satisfaction.' After the bridge was completed and railway traffic was crossing it continually without mishap, people's fears were to a large extent allayed, although from contemporary newspaper items one can sense a lurking unease.

The gale of Sunday 28 December, was of exceptional ferocity, newspapers describing numerous accidents; people blown off their feet; damage to buildings, tree plantations, railway wagons, telegraph-poles, etc. Ships were wrecked or driven ashore and streets strewn with debris. The Tayport lighthousekeeper reported that the wind had shaken the lantern, an event which had not occurred since a gale in 1859. A retired admiral from Fife asserted that several squalls had reached hurricane force, there being a particularly severe blast at about 7.20 p.m. which snapped off a walnut tree in his garden. From all parts the reports came in of a gale of almost unprecedented fury.

The gale struck Dundee about five o'clock in the evening though it did not reach its height until about two hours later. By six o'clock, the Tay Bridge Station had lost most of its roof and three loaded coal wagons had been blown out of a siding and carried along for some 400 yards. The 5.50 p.m. train from Newport to Dundee set out as normal, but experienced a tremendous buffeting as it crossed the bridge. Sparks flew out from the wheels, caused by their flanges being pushed tight against the rails by the force of the wind, and the carriages rocked from side to side as they were struck by several terrific gusts. Nonetheless the train reached the far side of the bridge safely, but disaster was awaiting the next train to cross.

The ill-fated train was bound from Burntisland to Dundee and consisted of an engine, a brake-van and six coaches. Seventy-one passengers were on board and four railwaymen – driver, stoker, guard and mail-guard. After leaving St Fort station, the train arrived at the signal cabin at the south end of the bridge at its normal time, 7.13 p.m. It slowed down to a walking pace so that the signalman could hand the driver the 'train staff' (a baton) without which the train could not cross the bridge; he then returned to his cabin and signalled the train on to the cabin at the north end of the bridge.

In the meantime James Black Lawson of Dundee was making his way eastwards along Magdalen Green with a friend, David Smart, the men being curious to see whether the Burntisland train would venture out on to the bridge during the gale. The wind was whipping the surface of the river into white foam and sheets of spray were blowing right over the bridge. The lights of the train appeared at the south end of the bridge and the men watched as they moved out across it, but about half-way over the lights were suddenly extinguished, and the men saw what appeared to be a mass of burning coals fall from the bridge near the Dundee end of the high girders. They could see nothing very clearly as clouds were flying across the moon, but certain that some sort of accident had occurred they ran across the Green, seeking shelter under one of the landward spans of the bridge. Here they found a group of men, some of whom had also seen the shower of fire falling towards the river. One of them, George Clark, had binoculars but they were useless in the flying spray, so Clark and Lawson made their way along the esplanade to a point where it was overlooked by the north signal-box. They tried to attract the signalman's attention but their voices were drowned by the wind, so they began to climb the steps up to the box. Henry Somerville, the signalman, saw them and came down, but even close together they could not hear each other over the roar of the gale. They sought the shelter of the railway arch where Lawson asked Somerville where the train was, but the latter, who had apparently seen nothing in the darkness, could only reply that it must be taking a long time to come off the bridge. Lawson and Clark then ran along the esplanade to Tay Bridge Station where they collided with James Smith, the stationmaster, and a guard leaving Smith's office. They knew that the train had started over the bridge and were becoming increasingly anxious as it failed to arrive. They had tried to contact the south signal-box by telegraph but when they could not get through concluded that the wires had been blown down. Lawson and Clark breathlessly recounted what they had seen, but Smith was still not convinced that the train was lost, suggesting that it might have stopped and gone back to the south side. He instructed everyone to say nothing until there was definite news and ordered the staff to close the station and shut the gates.

Lawson ran off to the harbour offices, Clark made his way to the office of the ferry superintendent and Smith went in search of James Roberts, the Locomotive Superintendent of the North

Britain Railway Company at Dundee, whom he found at the
engine shed. The two latter hurried to the north signal-box to talk
to signalman Somerville who reported that the train was signalled
to him from the south signal-box; that it had proceeded on to the
bridge at 7.14, and that he had looked out of his cabin at 7.22 to
see if it were approaching. There being no sign of it, he had tried
to telephone and then telegraph the south signal-box but was
unable to get through. The only way to find out what had
happened was to go out on to the bridge. The stationmaster and
locomotive superintendent bravely struggled on to the bridge in the
ferocious gale and groped their way along in almost total darkness,
soaked by spray from the river and often forced to their hands and
knees by the strength of the wind. For stationmaster Smith the
ordeal became too much: his head spinning, he stayed where he
was, clinging to the handrail, while his colleague pressed on.
Finally, over half a mile out on the bridge, Roberts arrived at the
last of the low spans, where he should have been able to see the
high girders, but there was nothing. Going a few yards further, he
saw a yawning gap where the middle girders had gone, and down
below the surging waves breaking over something in the river. To
add to the turmoil, the water-main which the bridge carried was
broken and gushing water was being blown into spray by the gale.
Horrified at what he had seen, Superintendent Roberts laboriously
made his way back along the bridge with the terrible news, but all
still clung to the faint hope that, even though the bridge had gone,
the train might just have had time to turn back. Roberts made his
way to the harbour office to see if a boat could be got out and
Smith returned to the station to telegraph the news to the North
Britain head office in Edinburgh.

While these tragic events were taking place, the harbourmaster,
Captain Robertson was leaving church about 8.00 p.m. to find the
streets littered with debris. At about 7.15, the minister had
momentarily halted his sermon as a particularly loud gust seemed
to threaten the church roof. As he reached the end of the street,
the harbourmaster and others of the congregation were met by an
excited man, who told them that the bridge was down, whereupon
Captain Robertson hurried to Tay Bridge Station. Smith and
Roberts had still not returned from the bridge with the dire news,
but from his office the horrified harbourmaster saw through his
telescope that the middle section was missing. Leaving his office he
went on to the esplanade, where many people were now gathering.

There was also a crowd at the station, many desperately seeking
information concerning relatives who were on the train. Some

clung to the chance that the train was still safe. It was known that it was fitted with the Westinghouse brake, which would have stopped it in a very short distance, and some suggested that the violent application of the brakes could have caused the sparks which had been seen, and possibly the failure of the train's lights. All were stunned by the swift, silent, tragedy – no noise had been heard above the roar of the storm.

There was still no news from the south end of the bridge: the telegraph and telephone lines were down, and the steam ferryboat, *Dundee*, could not cross the Tay for the gale force winds. Finally, however, at about nine o'clock, the gale had abated somewhat and the *Dundee* set out across the firth, returning an hour later: nothing was known at Newport, and the winds and currents had prevented her approaching close to the bridge. In the mean time, the postmaster at Dundee had received a telegram from the post office at Broughty Ferry, reporting that several mailbags from the train, and other wreckage, had been washed ashore; final, indisputable proof, that the train had indeed plunged into the river.

Even at this late stage it was hoped that there might be some survivors, perhaps clinging to pieces of wreckage in the water, and the *Dundee*, with food and blankets aboard, set out. Struggling against the wind she finally got to within a hundred yards of the bridge and the damage could be clearly seen. Not one of the thirteen large girders which spanned the navigable part of the river remained, the masonry piers sticking up like broken tree stumps above the water. For an instant it looked as if there might be people clinging to some of the piers, but the 'people' were pieces of ironwork. It was too dangerous to take the *Dundee* any closer; a boat was lowered and rowed between the piers and as close to the girders as possible, but there were no survivors and no trace of the train. Nothing further could be done that night and it was arranged that the steam-tug *Fairweather* should set out with divers at 7.30 next morning, when low tide would make diving operations easier.

Strangely, some fifty miles from Dundee, a 'crisis apparition' seems to have been experienced by a farmer as he was driving home from evening service with an elder of the Free Church of Prestonpans. Suddenly a terrific gust of wind struck the vehicle and the farmer exclaimed 'My God!' 'What's the matter,' asked his friend, 'Are you ill?' 'No, no, I'm not ill,' came the reply, 'but the Tay Bridge is down! I *saw* it!'

Next day, as dawn broke, thousands of people flocked to Magdalen Green to view the scene of the disaster. The storm had blown itself out, to be followed by a clear morning, with hardly a ripple on the water, and diving operations had already begun. By midday, news of the disaster had travelled around the world: the nation was stunned, and Queen Victoria sent a message to the Provost of Dundee, deploring the tragedy and asking for up-to-date news.

At about nine o'clock that morning, the first of the bodies was taken from the water near the beach east of Taygrove, near Newport. It was that of a woman, Ann Cruickshanks, aged about sixty. Bodies continued to be recovered over the following few months, one being washed up as far north as Ulbster on the Caithness coast, but the remains of many victims were never recovered. The salvage work continued for the next four months, pieces of the iron latticework and wreckage from the train being laboriously located, disentangled and brought to the surface and the engine was finally beached at Newport in April.

Several witnesses described how they had seen the fall of the train. James Phin, a Dundee grocer, was talking with two friends at his home at the time the train was due to cross the bridge, and one of them suggested that they go to an upstairs window to see it make the journey. They lowered the gas-lamp in the room to see the train lights more distinctly and watched the train as it went out on to the bridge. Then they saw two bright flashes and all the lights disappeared. Realizing immediately that something terrible had happened, they rushed down to the esplanade below the signal-box where they met James Lawson and the others.

Another witness described in the *Dundee Advertiser* how he and his family had seen the train fall. The gale was howling and chimney-pots were falling and smashing into the streets when, startled by a particularly loud crash, he went to the window and, as the clouds cleared for a moment, saw the Tay Bridge brightly illuminated by the moonlight. Almost instinctively he reached for his watch and, seeing it was seven o'clock, said to his wife, 'The Edinburgh train will be due immediately. Come and let us watch to see if it will attempt to cross on such a night.' (The train, known locally as 'the Edinburgh', actually started from Burntisland, where it picked up passengers from Edinburgh who were ferried across the firth from Granton to Burntisland, thence to Dundee.) The gas was turned down and the family gathered at the window. The witness continues:

The light by this time had become most fitful. Great masses of clouds were scouring across the expanse of the heavens, at times totally obscuring the light of the full moon; but occasionally the sky became clear ... 'There she comes!', cried one of the children, and at that moment the slowly moving lights of the Edinburgh train could be distinctly seen rounding the curve at Wormit, and, passing the signal box at the south side, enter upon the long straight line of that part of the bridge. The train once on the bridge seemed to move with great swiftness along, and when the engine entered the tunnel-like cloisters of the great girders my little girl exactly described the effects of the light as seen through the lattice work when she exclaimed, 'Look, papa, isn't that like lightning?' All this takes some time to write down, but to the eye it seemed as if almost simultaneous with the entrance of the train upon this part of the bridge, a comet-like burst of fiery sparks sprang out as if forcibly ejected into the darkness from the engine. In a long visible trail the streak of fire was seen till quenched in the stormy water below. Then there was absolute darkness on the bridge. A silence fell upon the eager group at the window. Then with stunning force the idea broke upon my mind. 'Heavens!', I cried, 'I fear the train is over the bridge.'

The witness snatched up his hat and rushed down to Magdalen

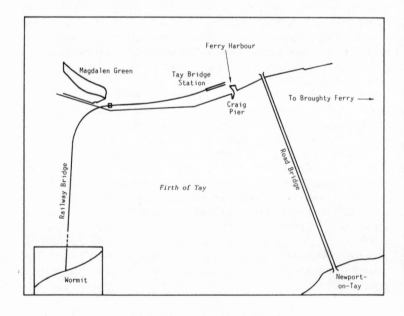

Fig. 14. Dundee and the Tay Bridge

Green, being forced, when descending the slope of the green, to crouch down on the grass to avoid being blown over. He joined the others on the esplanade and looked out over the river. A huge gap seemed to have been made in the bridge but it was hard to make anything out in the darkness. Eventually, as the storm abated, he made his way home, feeling, he said, 'overpowering gloom and sadness'.

What force did the wind reach that night? It has been estimated that the mean wind speed was 60 m.p.h. with gusts of up to 80 m.p.h. A wind of more than 73 m.p.h. is classed as a hurricane, so that it is probable that the Tay Bridge was toppled by gusts of at least hurricane force. It is even possible that a short-lived tornado had developed. Consider the testimony of W.B. Thomson, an engineer and shipbuilder at the Caledon Shipyard at Dundee. He had attended the service at the Free Church at Broughty Ferry on the Sunday night, noting that it was 7.06 when the congregation left the church. He walked down to the beach to see what the river looked like in the gale, but found it impossible to turn the corner at the sea-front because of the sand and pebbles that were whirling about. He sheltered at the corner of James Place for about fifteen minutes, and later reported:

While there, I distinctly saw two luminous columns of mist or spray travelling across the river in the direction of the wind. Another one formed directly in front of me just in an instant. It appeared to rise from the centre of the river. I never saw anything like it before, and looked round to see if anyone was near me, but seeing nobody thought it was better to take shelter. I went inside the railing in front of James Place and held on by one of them thinking that the column, which was advancing towards me, was to carry everything before it. It passed over me. It was spray from the river, not solid water. It struck the house behind me with a hissing noise. The height of each of these columns I should think was 250 to 300 feet. On the following morning I found the windows of my house (about 170 feet above the river) coated with salt. I never saw this before in a westerly wind, and can only account for this by one of these columns passing over the house. My theory is that the north end of the bridge gave way first, the failure being caused by one such column rising or passing under it. Such a thing would tend to lift the girders from their piers; or the wind, which had the effect of lifting that column of spray, had also the effect of raising the girders from the piers, thereby overcoming part of the resistance offered to the lateral pressure of the wind.

Ex-provost William Robertson who lived at Newport, also saw two

huge columns of spray in the river at the time the bridge went
down. He could only assume that they had been caused by
wreckage falling into the water, but Mr Thomson thought that
such tall columns of spray could not be generated in such a
manner, and believed them to be the same phenomenon that he
had encountered.

Work on the new Tay Bridge was begun in 1881, the piers of the
new structure being built exactly in line with those of the old which
were left in position to act as cutwaters; these can be seen today.
The remaining girders of the old bridge were perfectly sound so
they were transferred to the piers of the new bridge, an extra set of
girders then being added to allow the second Tay Bridge to carry
two sets of railway lines. It was opened on 11 July 1887 and stands
to this day.

There was not a single survivor of the Tay Bridge disaster, but it
can be said that the death toll would have been much worse if it
had not occurred on a Sunday evening, when relatively few people
were travelling, and that, like similar disasters, it provided lessons
for designers and engineers. This tragedy has an epic, timeless
quality, with features reminiscent of the loss of the *Titanic* – proud
achievements destroyed like toys by natural forces.

The Fastnet Storm, 1979

The first Fastnet Yacht Race, from Cowes, past the Isles of Scilly,
round the Fastnet Rock off the south-west coast of Ireland and
back, was held in 1925. Since then it has taken place in alternate
Augusts, and until 1979 was remarkably free of casualties, the only
fatality having occurred in 1931. Since a gale in 1957, when only
twelve of the forty-one competitors completed the course, the
weather has generally been good for the Fastnet Race, but on the
night of 13/14 August 1979 a severe depression brought
storm-force winds and forty-foot waves to the Irish Sea, with tragic
consequences for the Fastnet fleet.

The yachts, 302 in number, with 3,000 crew had set sail from
Cowes at 1.50 p.m. on Saturday 11 August, the weather being fair,
with a light westerly wind, a fairly high barometer and the nearest
potential for bad weather a depression over Nova Scotia. The race
proceeded uneventfully until Monday evening, by which time most
of the craft had passed the Scilly Isles and headed out into the Irish
Sea. The midday weather forecast warned of force six to eight
winds that night but this brought no great alarm to the contestants,
many of whom had experienced winds of this strength. As night
drew on, however, it became apparent that the winds were going

to be far in excess of force eight; the depression over Nova Scotia had moved rapidly across the Atlantic and deepened, and the shipping forecast at 12.15 a.m. on Tuesday 14 August predicted winds of force nine and ten but some crews were to encounter winds of force eleven during the following hours.

The experience of the 37-foot *Trophy* is typical of the ordeals some of the crews suffered that night. *Trophy* was captained by Alan Bartlett, a 53-year-old publican and the brother-in-law of comedian Eric Morecambe. He had been a keen amateur sailor for twenty-five years. His crew consisted of Simon Fleming, a 26-year-old director of a Surrey heating firm; Robin Bowyer, a 42-year-old youth-sailing-instructor from Farnborough; Peter Everson, an executive for a Billericay car firm in his early thirties; John Puxley, forty-two, a crane-driver from Burnham-on-Crouch; Richard Mann, a 30-year-old London plasterer; 22-year old Russell Smith, a London company director; and Derek Morland, a precision turner from Southampton. They had competed in five of the Cowes Week events, but had only completed two of the races. They were looking forward with great excitement to the Fastnet Race.

On the Monday morning the *Trophy* was becalmed off Lands End, but she made good progress as the winds freshened, and by 8 p.m. was being swept along by a wind of about 36 m.p.h. The crew struggled on as the wind grew stronger, though some of them managed to take a sleep below. At 11 p.m. the crew saw a red distress flare, and Alan Bartlett gave the order to turn towards it: with the wind howling and blowing a blinding horizontal spray, the crew of the *Trophy* searched in the darkness for a vessel in distress. At last a light appeared, and then a dismasted boat was seen wallowing helplessly in the waves. At this point an escort boat, *Morningtown*, a 39-foot motor/sailer, appeared out of the darkness to help the yacht, so the *Trophy* withdrew. At midnight Robin Bowyer tuned in the boat's radio to the weather forecast to hear that a force ten gale was imminent, and it was shortly after this that the first great wave, described by Simon Fleming as 'a wall of water' crashed on to the yacht, forcing her backwards through the water and breaking her rudder. The crew, after recovering from the shock, attempted to repair her steering equipment but to no avail, and they resigned themselves to riding out the storm until morning. Fleming, Bowyer, Puxley, Mann and Morland went below to their bunks, leaving Bartlett and the others on deck. It was then that the second wave struck, and this time the boat turned over, trapping those below in a tangle of ropes, sails and

floorboards. The yacht slowly righted herself and the men fought
clear of the debris and clambered up on to the deck. The mast had
been smashed and the rigging was a tangle. Rather than risk the
boat turning over again, it was decided to abandon ship and take
their chance in the liferaft.

One by one the crew lowered themselves over the edge of the
yacht and into the rubber liferaft, the rope was cut and the tiny
craft paddled away. The liferaft was battered mercilessly by the
wind and waves, losing its stabilizing sea-anchor and its entire
upper section, including its upper buoyancy ring. Wave after wave
crashed on to it, washing the men off several times. Each time they
managed to scramble back into it, but they were growing weaker
and finally John Puxley and Peter Everson were carried away. The
others tried frantically to paddle the raft towards them, but it was
hopeless in the enormous waves and the two men were lost from
sight. Shortly after, as dawn broke, the raft split into two parts,
leaving Fleming in one while the remaining five men lay in the
water clinging to the other; the sections drifted apart and Robin
Bowyer began to succumb to cold and exhaustion. The others tried
to keep him afloat and conscious, but to no avail. 'It was apparent
that he was going,' said Bartlett later, 'and he actually died there.
Before he slipped away he was dead.' Bartlett himself felt that he
could hold on no longer, but then he heard a helicopter overhead,
and the men began frantically to wave and shout. A Dutch
destroyer also appeared on the scene. Bartlett and Fleming were
air-lifted into the helicopter, the other three being taken aboard
the destroyer.

Most of the damage to boats took place in the area of the
Labadie Bank, situated about half-way between Land's End and
the Fastnet Rock, and about thirty miles long. The depth of water
over this bank is between 200 and 300 feet, and considerably less
than the rest of the Channel and this produced a more confused
and steeper wave formation.

One of the boats which met disaster over the Labadie Bank was
the 35-foot *Allamanda*, skippered by Michael Campbell. She was
dismasted and rolled over through 180 degrees and then righted
herself, with the crew hanging on by their lifelines. When a
helicopter appeared at 6.30 p.m. on Tuesday 14 August, they
decided to abandon ship and were lifted to safety.

Morning Cloud, skippered by Edward Heath, was rolled over
through 90 degrees when rounding the Fastnet Rock at 2.15 on
Tuesday morning but she righted herself and the crew, thrown
about and bruised, went on to finish the course.

The official finish of the race was 16 August, when the figures were: 302 boats started, 194 retired, 85 finished, 23 abandoned of which 5 sank. Fifteen crew were drowned and 136 rescued.

Rescue services were stretched to their limits that night. Helicopter pilots from the Royal Navy's air station at Culdrose in Cornwall were working round the clock bringing men ashore from abandoned yachts, and a plea was sent out for helicopter crewmen on leave to return to duty immediately. During the morning of Tuesday the four Sea King helicopters were joined by two Wessex helicopters, and the RAF sent three long-range Nimrod jets to the area. The Dutch destroyer, *Overijssel*, which had been escorting the fleet, was joined by the fishery protection vessel HMS *Anglesey* and the frigate HMS *Broadsword*, which was sent from Plymouth with medical supplies. Two naval tugs, *Rollicker* and *Robust*, also joined the rescue fleet. Culdrose air station was overwhelmed with telephone calls from anxious relatives, calling from all parts of Britain, the United States, New Zealand and Singapore. Also taking part in rescue attempts were several lifeboats, including three from Irish stations, and several trawlers which happened to be in the area.

Records of the Meteorological Office indicate that deep depressions, carrying storm force winds, appear in the South-west Approaches, on average, once in ten years.

An enquiry into the Fastnet Race disaster was held by the Royal Yachting Association and the Royal Ocean Racing Club, and the main conclusion was that the blame for the calamity should be placed on the severity of the storm. The enquiry also expressed the opinion: 'However, provided that the lessons so harshly taught in this race are well learnt, we feel that yachts should continue to race over the Fastnet course.'

Strange Accident at New Cross

A severe south-westerly gale was the cause of one of the strangest accidents on Britain's railways, which occurred in 1863, at the engine sheds of the London, Brighton and South Coast Railway at New Cross, South London.

On the afternoon of Friday 30 October, work was proceeding as normal in one of the engine sheds with fitters, firemen and drivers working around the locomotives. Four or five engines were raising steam, with two ready to leave when, at about 3.40, without any warning, a terrific gust of wind blasted into the open end of the shed and, unable to escape from the confined space, blew off the roof which then collapsed bringing down the walls. The shed was a substantial structure – 145 feet wide with 14-inch brick walls reinforced every 21 feet by 23-inch thick piers – yet in a matter of seconds it was reduced to rubble.

The collapse of the building was accompanied by a deafening rumbling which brought Joseph Craven, assistant locomotive superintendent rushing out of his office. He was confronted by a scene of appalling confusion, later described by the *Kentish Mercury* as follows:

> The demolition of the place was complete, and there was nothing to be seen but a confused mass of bricks, broken beams and coke, heavy iron girders and rods sticking up here and there, engines overturned, and the whole enveloped in steam from the broken engines.

One of the walls, against the outside of which were stacked hundreds of tons of coke, had fallen inwards, while the other had collapsed outwards, completely blocking the rails of the Croydon line. Pieces of timber and slates from the roof had been hurled for a distance of some sixty yards around. Mr Craven frantically waved his arms to stop all traffic and then rushed over to the ruins of the shed. The men had fled for their lives at the first alarm, but several had been buried in the rubble. One man, Henry William Woodrow, had been killed outright and was found with a broken back, his thighs smashed and terrible head injuries. Three others, George Cutts, William Smith and Charles Privett, were seriously injured and were taken to Guy's Hospital. The other men, about a dozen in number, escaped with cuts and bruises.

One description of the scene of devastation came from Alfred Rosling Bennett, a boy at the time of the accident, who later described it as one of the most vivid recollections of his youth. In his book *Historic Locomotives and Moving Accidents by Steam and Rail*, he reported:

> About 4.25 on the afternoon of 30th October, 1863, while a terrific south-west gale was raging, I arrived at New Cross by the 4.15 West Croydon train from London Bridge. As my train entered New Cross I was amazed to perceive that one of the two big engine-sheds which in the morning had stood at the end of the up slow platform was no longer visible, and that in its place stood a crowd of men round a mass of ruins on the top of 7 or 8 locomotives.
>
> Before the train had stopped I was out and over the line, just pausing to let a down fast South Eastern train, drawn by a 'Jimmy Sharp' engine, whistling at full blast, pass. Everybody was too busy to notice a boy, and I was able to watch the dismal scene at my ease.

A dead man had just been laid on a stretcher and reverently covered up; and later several badly injured men – I heard it whispered that one had a broken back – were placed on stretchers and carried away. The engines were battered, dented and covered with dust, bricks, coke, slates and beams, but the worst injured was No.111 which had been knocked off the line and lay partly in the ash-pit over which it had been standing. Water was being played into the fire-box from a hose ...

The inquest into the death of Henry Woodrow was held on Monday 2 November, at the Railway Tavern, New Cross, under the direction of Coroner W. Carter. Mr Edward Bowyer Giles, a tailor from Middlesex, identified the body as that of his nephew, who was single and twenty-three years old. John White, an engine-driver, said that during the gale he was working at the front of his engine (No. 111), Henry Woodrow being engaged in tightening a nut near the buffer of the engine on the right side. At about 3.30 he saw pieces of coke and dirty waste, used in cleaning the engines blowing about at the front of the shed, then a great gust of wind came into the building and he saw the roof lift up. White, with a fireman and a fitter, scrambled underneath the engine, scarcely gaining shelter before there was a crash and the engine came down on top of them. Just prior to this he had seen the deceased leaning over the buffer of the engine with his back to the wall. If the engine had settled any lower, said White, he and his colleagues would certainly have been crushed to death. Later, he saw the deceased bent forward with his head towards the engine pit, jammed in with masonry from the fallen wall. There was blood on his head and face and when released he was dead. The inquest brought in a verdict of 'Accidental Death'.

The Falling Towers of Ferrybridge
Countless man-made structures have succumbed to the force of the wind, the age-old enemy of the civil engineer, perhaps the most famous British example being that of the Tay Bridge. It is rare, however, that such accidents are captured by the camera, but on Monday 1 November, 1965, a dramatic photograph was taken of the destruction of a huge cooling tower at Ferrybridge Power Station in Yorkshire during a north-westerly gale.

Construction of the enormous power-station, which is situated about a mile north-west of Knottingley, was begun in 1961 and the station, at the time the largest in Western Europe, was still incomplete when disaster struck. Two thousand five hundred people worked at the site, on which there were two chimneys 660 feet high and eight cooling towers arranged in two parallel, staggered rows 350 feet apart. Each tower was 375 feet high, 300 feet across the base, and 180 feet across at the top, the narrower 'throat' having a diameter of 165 feet; they were made of reinforced concrete five inches thick.

The gale that morning caused widespread damage in Yorkshire; houses were damaged, roads blocked by fallen masonry and high-sided vehicles blown over, but there seemed no cause for alarm at the power-station. At 10.30, however, tower 1B majestically collapsed, to be followed ten minutes later by tower 1A. The power station chemist had grabbed his camera and dashed outside after the first tower had fallen; he aimed his camera and photographed the second tower as it tumbled to the ground, only to discover that in his hurry he had left his lens cap on, but he did succeed in photographing the third tower, 2A, which collapsed some forty minutes later at 11.20 a.m. Witnesses have described how it became plastic and undulated like a sail in the wind, rippling just below the throat, then flexing 'as if a man was standing inside a bell tent and passing his hand horizontally round the inside of the fabric.' A hole appeared in the side of the tower, the top fell forward and the sides caved in.

A reporter from the *Pontefract and Castleford Express* arrived at the scene shortly after the collapse of the third tower, and he described the wreckage on the site as the gale raged:

> We were at times lifted off our feet by the wind, as we reached the lee side of the shattered shells and saw the jumble of wood-work within the remnants. Twice I was whipped completely off my feet by the force of gusts.
>
> A big jib crane swung, deserted, over a litter of huts some of which had 'caught it' as the towers fell ... a burst water pipe sprayed. Floodwater and powdered concrete whipped and stung our faces. Rain squalls came, drowning out the sun. And all the while a high-pitched screaming, as of wind in tortured wire, put talking out of the question ... As we sought to get into position to take photographs there came a crack like a field-gun and I thought attempts must be under way to blast down another tower. Then the cause of the noise became obvious as another crack brought down a great lightning flash, puff of smoke and a discharge from a pylon overhead. Something, perhaps wind-blow debris, had apparently touched the high tension wires ...

As the reporter and his colleagues left the site later they met a workman who described how he had heard a booming, roaring noise before the third tower fell. As it collapsed he and his workmates fled, and although they were more than a hundred yards from the falling tower the blast hit them like a hammer and huge pieces of debris flew past. Miraculously no one was seriously hurt at the site, though three received treatment at Pontefract Infirmary for minor injuries.

A fourth tower was said to have been cracked and there were fears that it would suffer the same fate as the other three. A battery of pressmen waited with cameras at the ready, but the tower resisted the gale and no more photographs were obtained.

The gale of 1 November 1965 was not of exceptional severity so why did the dramatic collapse occur? The Committee of Inquiry was satisfied that the construction, workmanship and materials were of a sufficiently high standard. The Ferrybridge cooling towers had been designed to the standard allowance for wind-speed.

The average wind-speed at Ferrybridge that morning was estimated at 67 m.p.h. at a height of 400 feet, with minute-long gusts of 75 m.p.h. However, after the disaster it was calculated that there had been gusts, lasting only three seconds perhaps, of up to 103 m.p.h., and it was these, smashing into the towers, which had caused them to collapse. Eighty-six years after the Tay Bridge catastrophe the power of such gusts had still not been appreciated. The committee was advised that such wind speeds might be expected to occur on average once every five years, and it was further estimated that once every fifty years gusts at a height of 400 feet could reach speeds of 118 m.p.h. It was also demonstrated that the siting of the towers had contributed to their collapse – their close proximity to each other would have channelled and increased the wind-speed and there would have been much eddying and turbulence.

7   Hurricanes

Daniel Defoe's Great Storm
The British Isles have been battered by many tremendous gales over the centuries, but there seems little doubt that the worst in recorded history was that of 26/27 November 1703. The gale killed more people, on land and sea, and destroyed more property than any other known storm before or since; the wind, it seems, blew at much more than hurricane force (which is 73–81 m.p.h. on the Beaufort Scale) for a considerable period. We owe most of our knowledge of this great tempest to Daniel Defoe (1660–1731) author of *Robinson Crusoe* and many other books and pamphlets. Only a few months before the storm Defoe had fallen foul of the authorities with a seditious pamphlet entitled *The Shortest Way with the Dissenters*, for which he was placed in the pillory. It is recorded, however, that a sympathetic crowd drank his health and pelted him with flowers rather than the usual rotten eggs and rubbish. After such hectic events he was probably glad to turn his talent to the safe, non-political subject of the Great Storm. His approach was similar to that of modern-day writers: he appealed for information in the newspapers of the day and added his own commentary to the many dramatic reports he received. Reading his book today one is indeed struck by the up-to-date style. Written in an age often regarded as credulous and superstitious, Defoe's work seems remarkably cautious and meticulous: he continually stresses the need for accuracy when dealing with reports of the hurricane and states that he has omitted all that appears improbable or fantastic and advances his own explanations for events which seem curious or inexplicable. Allowing for an inevitable quaintness of style, his account could have been written in the twentieth century rather than the eighteenth.

In the winter of 1703 there had been gale force winds for about two weeks before the hurricane itself; tiles blown from houses, chimneys falling and several ships wrecked, and as November progressed the worse the weather became. At about four o'clock on Wednesday 24 November, the wind suddenly increased in force, with terrific gusts, Defoe himself having a narrow escape when part of a house crashed down near him. The gales continued through Thursday and Friday, but still did not cause any general apprehension. The first intimation of the impending disaster came on the Friday evening, when it was noticed that barometric pressure had fallen to an exceptionally low level. In fact Defoe did not believe the reading on his own barometer, thinking that his children had been tampering with it. Still, most people went to bed as usual, and it was not until the early hours of the morning of the 27th that it became obvious that Britain was at the mercy of a hurricane of unprecedented violence. People feared their homes would collapse around them, but dared not go outside as the streets were full of flying debris – pieces of timber, sheets of iron and lead, bricks, slates and tiles. Defoe records seeing heavy tiles blown thirty or forty yards and embedded up to eight inches in hard earth. The ferocity of the wind reached its peak in London at about 3.00 a.m. then slowly subsided, and by about eight o'clock next morning frightened folk began to peer out of their houses and take stock of the devastation which, said Defoe, was beyond description. Of London, he wrote:

> Indeed the city was a strange spectacle, the morning after the storm, as soon as people could put their heads out of doors; though I believe, everybody expected the destruction was bad enough; yet I question very much if anybody believed the hundredth part of what they saw.

Normal life was suspended in London for the next few days as people cleared away the debris, patched up their houses with odd bits of timber and tarpaulin, checked on the safety of friends and relatives, or simply wandered about, viewing the devastation. In some parts of London whole houses had been demolished, while others had lost roofs, walls, windows and chimneys. Falling chimney stacks presented one of the greatest hazards of the storm, crashing through roofs and floors and burying people under piles of rubble. Some twenty people in London met their deaths in this manner and many others were injured. Many public buildings lost roofs, slates and pinnacles, and part of St James's Palace collapsed. Thousands of trees were blown down in the parks, some, in St James's Park, reportedly having been planted by Cardinal Wolsey about two hundred years earlier. Surprisingly, there was little damage to London Bridge and the buildings on it,

Defoe speculating that this was due to the wind having been channelled under the arches of the bridge.

The cost of roofing materials immediately soared, the price of plain tiles rising from 21 shillings to £6 per thousand and that of pantiles from 50 shillings to £10 per thousand. Labour costs rose as well, bricklayers charging 5 shillings a day instead of the usual 2 shillings. Consequently many people decided to wait until prices fell before repairing their properties, either covering their roofs in the interim with wooden boards – Defoe comments that he had seen whole streets roofed in this manner – or simply leaving their roofs unrepaired and open to the elements.

Not everyone was cowering at home terrifed while the storm raged. Defoe records with a sense of horror that, at the very height of the storm, a 'gang of hardened rogues' broke into a house at Poplar, terrifying the occupants and stealing their belongings. The victims shouted 'thieves' and 'fire', but self-preservation was the order of the night, and no help was forthcoming.

How had the rest of the country fared? The centre of the storm seems to have passed over Liverpool, moving across England in an easterly direction, the strongest winds, as is often the case with such storms, being to the south of the storm centre. In fact the worst damage was caused south of a line drawn from the Bristol Channel to the Thames. In the West Country the storm seems to have been at its height at or before midnight; in London at about 3 a.m.; on the Downs an hour later and on the Dutch coast about daybreak at 7.30 a.m. Defoe rode round Kent after the storm surveying the damage, later reporting:

> The collector of these accounts cannot but enter the remarks he made, having occasion to traverse the county of Kent about a month after the storm; and besides the general desolation which in every village gave almost the same prospect, he declares that he reckoned 1107 dwelling-houses, out-houses and barns blown quite down, whole orchards of fruit trees laid flat upon the ground, and of all other sorts of trees such a quantity, that though he attempted to take an account of them, he found it was impossible, and was obliged to give it over.'

In fact, Defoe counted approximately 17,000 trees blown down in Kent before giving up. It is unlikely that much of the timber went to waste. Enormous quantities were needed to repair or rebuild houses, ships, barns and windmills. Churches suffered greatly in the gale, at least seven had their steeples blown down, and many others were badly damaged. The Reverend Samuel Farr, from

Stowmarket in Suffolk, described how the spire of his church, which had been rebuilt in 1674, was blown 'clean off' and travelled twenty-eight feet down the length of the church before smashing through the roof. The Reverend Thomas Figg of Brenchley in Kent reported that the steeple of his church, one of the tallest in Kent, was thrown down and 'made the sport and pastimes of boys and girls, who in future ages, tho' perhaps incredibly, yet can boast they leaped over such a steeple.' At the church of Fairford in Gloucestershire, two magnificent stained glass windows (one 25 feet high and 15 feet wide, and valued at over £1,500) were destroyed by the gale. One of the most bizarre effects of the wind was to strip the lead off roofs, as at Berkeley in Gloucester, where twenty-six sheets of lead, joined together, were blown from the middle aisle of the church clean over the north aisle and landed in the churchyard, thirty feet away from the building. Each sheet, it was estimated, weighed some 3½ cwt. At Leamington Hastings in Warwickshire, the roof of the middle aisle of the church was stripped of its lead, many of the sheets being rolled up like pieces of cloth. Six of the sheets, weighing together about 50 cwt, were blown to a distance of 150 yards, before hitting a tree, one of them being wrapped round the trunk. At Christchurch in Hampshire, according to one William Mitchell, twelve sheets of lead on the church roof were 'rouled up together, that 20 men could not have done the like, to the great amazement of those that saw 'em.' At Ewell, near Epsom in Surrey, the lead from the flat roof of a Mr Williams's house was rolled up by the wind and blown to a distance of approximately 120 yards from the house. The lead was estimated to weigh in the region of 10 tons.

At least 400 windmills were destroyed in the hurricane, some being blown over, others set on fire by the heat generated in the machinery by the furiously rotating sails. The miller of Charlewood Mill, near Reigate in Surrey, had a narrow escape. He rose from his bed with the intention of turning the sails of his mill into the wind, thus setting it in motion, and, he hoped, preventing it from being blown over. On his way to the mill, however, he discovered that he had forgotten the key and rushed back for it. Hastily returning, he found that he was too late, the mill had been blown over, but in forgetting the key he had saved his life. Not so fortunate were Dr Kidder, Bishop of Bath and Wells, and his wife who were killed when two chimneys smashed through the roof of their apartments. An account from J. Bagshot records bluntly:

> He perceived the fall before it came, and accordingly jump't out of bed, and made towards the door, where he was found with his

brains dashed out; his lady perceiving it, wrap't all the bed-clothes about her, and in that manner was found smothered in bed.

Probably the most famous casualty of the hurricane was Henry Winstanley, builder of the first Eddystone lighthouse. Innumerable ships had been wrecked on the Eddystone rock, a great chunk of granite, part of a submerged reef, some fourteen miles SSW of Plymouth, until in 1666, the year of the great plague, it was decided that a lighthouse should be built there. But still years went by and though some survey work was undertaken, nothing definite was accomplished until the interest of Henry Winstanley, an archetypal English eccentric with a quirkily inventive mind, was aroused. At his home at Littlebury in Essex, there were all manner of mechanical tricks and booby traps, such as a bench by the canal at the bottom of his garden, which would tip into the water anyone who sat upon it. To this unlikely civil engineer the task of building the lighthouse was entrusted.

Winstanley began work in 1695, laboriously securing the foundations of his lighthouse to the rock. He then built a masonry column, some twelve feet high and sixteen feet in diameter, which was surmounted by an eighty-foot high tower of wood and stone. The lantern was first lit on 14 November, 1698, but the tower proved too short, the light not being clearly visible and the waves sweeping right over it in stormy weather. Winstanley therefore enlarged the structure, widening the base to 24 feet and extending the tower to over 100 feet. It was finally finished in 1699 and presented a very bizarre appearance, the tower being festooned with weather vanes, derricks, galleries and pinnacles. It also had a movable chute on the top through which stones could be showered on approaching enemies, this perhaps being inspired by Winstanley's capture by a French privateer while he was working on the rock. The outside of the tower was painted with suns and compasses and mottoes, such as *Post Tenebras Lux* (After Darkness Light), and *Pax in Bello* (Peace in War), whilst, inside, in addition to a kitchen and accommodation for the keeper, there was an elegant stateroom, and a splendid bedchamber, richly painted and gilded.

Many people expressed their doubts that the structure would stand up to a severe gale, but Winstanley had complete confidence in his creation, saying that he would like to be in it during the greatest storm that had ever blown. His wish was granted: on 26 November 1703, following a lull in the bad weather, he went to the lighthouse with five men to carry out repairs. The next morning, after the gale, there was not the slightest trace of the wooden tower or its occupants. So perished Henry Winstanley who, for all his eccentricities, was a brave, clever and determined man. Defoe writes that on the night of his death a model of the lighthouse at his home in Littlebury fell over and was smashed to pieces.

Elsewhere there were some remarkable escapes: Mr Woodgate Giffer, from St Martin's Street, St Martin-in-the-Fields, London, reported:

> Between two and three of the clock in the morning, my neighbour's stack of chimneys fell, and broke down the roof of my garret into the passage going up and down stairs, upon which I thought it convenient to retire into the kitchen with my family, where we had not been above a quarter of an hour, before my wife sent her maid to fetch some necessaries out of the back parlour closet, and as she had shut the door and was upon her return, the very same instant my neighbour's stack of chimneys on the other side of the house, fell upon my stack, and beat in the roof, and so drove down the several floors through the parlour into the kitchen where the maid was buried near five hours in the rubbish, without the least damage or hurt whatsoever.

The hurricane seems to have been accompanied by other meteorological phenomena. For example, there were reports of thunder and lightning, Defoe commenting:

> And yet, though I cannot remember to have heard it thunder, or that I saw any lightning, or heard of any that did in or near London, yet in the country the air was seen full of meteors and vaporous fires: and in some places both thunderings and unusual flashes of lightning, to the great terror of the inhabitants.

In fact, one person, Joseph Clench, an apothecary from Jermyn Street, did report what seemed to be lightning in London, but the flashes, strangely, did not strike downwards but 'seemed rather to skim along the surface of the ground; nor did they appear to be of the same kind with the common lightning flashes.' Clench was also one of those who thought that there must have been an earthquake during the hurricane, noting that several springs in his neighbourhood were, for a period of about two days after the storm, very muddy, something he had never known after any other storms. He concluded that they could not be so affected 'by any thing less than a concussion of the earth itself.' Others insisted that they had actually felt an earthquake, though Defoe was sceptical, thinking that they had been misled by the wind buffeting their houses. Curiously, however, there was an undisputed earthquake in Yorkshire and Lincolnshire, just over a month later.

Another oddity, which preceded the hurricane by a few hours, was the tornado which was reported by the Reverend Joseph Ralton of Bessels Leigh, Oxon, described in more detail in Chapter 8.

At least 123 people were killed on land by the hurricane, but the losses at sea were far greater, it being estimated that 8,000 men were drowned, at least 1,500 of these in ships of the Royal Navy. The huge loss of life was because the great majority of ships were not out in the open sea where many might have ridden out the storm, but gathered together in anchorages such as Spithead, the Yarmouth Roads and the Downs. They had been sheltering in these roadsteads from the bad weather of the previous two weeks, some at the end of their journeys, waiting to enter harbour, and others outward bound. In the days of sail it was dangerous for ships to approach too close to land, or attempt to put into harbour in adverse weather conditions, for the risk of being blown ashore or wrecked, but in the sheltered anchorages ships could ride out storms and put to sea as soon as the weather changed. (Right up to the end of the last century it was a common sight to see as many as 400 ships collected in the Downs, waiting for a fair wind.) However, in the exceptional gale of 1703 the roadsteads provided no safe haven. The greatest losses occurred in the Downs, where some 160 merchant ships and several men-of-war, including the *Mary*, the *Northumberland*, the *Restoration* and the *Stirling Castle*, had gathered. On the night of the 26th the general direction of the wind was south-westerly, but at the time of its greatest force it blew a little more from the west, towards the notorious Goodwin Sands, where innumerable ships had been wrecked. The worst of the gale struck the ships at about one o'clock on the morning of the 27th, driving many of them out to sea, sinking others at their anchors, and wrecking at least twelve on the Goodwins, including the four warships mentioned. Many small ships, perhaps drawing only twelve feet of water, were blown right over the Goodwins, but for the larger ships there was no such escape. A fifth warship, the *Prince George*, ninety guns, rode out the gale, rather surprisingly as she was the only three-decked ship, and consequently the most top-heavy, in the Downs. She had been in danger from the smaller *Restoration*, which had dragged her anchors and come down upon her; the crews succeeded in keeping them apart, but the *Restoration* was blown over and wrecked.

Many sailors who had survived the destruction of their ships in

the Downs spent the night clinging to wreckage, and at low tide
next morning managed to crawl on to the Goodwin Sands, where
they could be seen through glasses from the mainland, frantically
signalling for help. They knew that in a few hours, when the tide
rose, the sands would again be covered. There now began one of
the most amazing episodes of the storm: several boats indeed went
out from Deal, not to save the shipwrecked sailors, but to salvage
booty from the wrecks. Their owners set about filling them with
plunder, ignoring the cries of the stranded men who almost
certainly would have been left to drown if it had not been for the
efforts of Thomas Powell, the Mayor of Deal. He was horrified by
the plight of the shipwrecked men and, being brusquely refused all
help from the Customs House officers, he rallied the local men and
offered to pay 5s. per head for all the sailors whose lives they could
save. More than 200 men, naked and half-dead with cold and
hunger, were brought ashore. The mayor now made an appeal to
the Queen's Agent for help and was again refused, the latter
stating that his duty was to assist seamen wounded in battle, and
not shipwrecked sailors. He therefore provided food, shelter,
travelling expenses and even burial costs from his own pocket. He
received no thanks or recognition from the government for this
humanitarian work, and it was only after repeated efforts that he
obtained recompense for his outlay, plus a small additional sum
for his heroic work in rescuing the stranded seamen. It was shortly
after this that a decree was made placing shipwrecked sailors in the
same category as those killed or wounded in action, their widows
and children receiving entitlement to a pension.

Several ships were blown across the North Sea to the continent,
one of these being the *Association*, a three-deck, ninety-gun
warship under the command of Vice-Admiral Sir Stafford
Fairborne. The English fleet, commanded by Admiral Sir
Cloudesley Shovell, returning from its summer campaign against
the French in the Mediterranean, had, after a stormy passage,
arrived in the Downs on 17 November. Several ships, including the
Prince George, were to remain there till the weather allowed them
to return to Portsmouth, while the admiral was ordered to sail to
Chatham with the remainder of the fleet, comprising seven
three-decker, one two-decker and several smaller craft. In those
days the main ship channel into the Thames and the Medway was
from the north-east, down along the Essex coast, vessels having to
go as far north as Harwich before making the turn to the
south-west. Sir Cloudesley Shovell's fleet accordingly proceeded
north from the Downs, and anchored at the Long Sand Head,

some fifteen miles off Harwich, to wait for a wind to take them down into the Medway. It was here that the hurricane struck them, four of the great ships, including the *Association*, being driven out to sea. She was dangerously close to the Galloper Sand, but at about 5 a.m. passed over the tail of the Galloper in about seven fathoms (42 feet) of water. Her ordeal was just beginning, for a tremendous sea smashed over her starboard side, breaking in the gunports of her upper deck, the mass of water thus entering causing her to heel dangerously. She probably would not have risen again had not the crew cut holes in the decks, allowing the water to run down to the hold where it could be pumped out. However, an enormous volume of water gathered on the lower gun deck and, surging to and fro, smashed open two of the gunports. This could easily have been the end of the ship, for the lower gun deck was only three feet above water-line when the ship was upright, but the crew managed to secure the ports and, against all odds, the ship survived. The *Association*'s adventures were still not over, the gale driving her across to Flanders, and then along the coast to the mouth of the Elbe where, on 4 December, she was battered by another storm which threatened to drive her ashore. A member of the crew later reported:

> We must all have inevitably perished, had not God mercifully favoured us about 10 o'clock at night with a south-west wind, which gave us an opportunity to put to sea. But being afterwards driven near the coast of Norway, the ship wanting anchors and cables, our wood and candles wholly expended: no beer on board, nor anything else in lieu; everyone reduced to one quart of water per day, the men, who had been harassed at Belle Isle, and in our Mediterranean voyage, now jaded by the continual fatigues of the storms, falling sick every day, the vice-admiral in this exigency thought it advisable to put into Gothenburg.

They docked at Gothenburg on 11 December where repairs were hastily carried out, and then went on to Copenhagen, where provisions were laid in. She sailed for home, accompanied by twelve merchant ships, on 3 January; just a few more days in port could have resulted in her being frozen in and a Scandinavian winter could have proved fatal to her already weakened crew. As it was, twenty-five men died before the ship reached home. More bad weather was encountered on the return trip, and four French privateers, attempting to seize some of the stores ships, had to be driven off, but finally, two months after the hurricane, the *Association* arrived in the Medway. Three of the other ships which had been blown across the channel had also reached the Dutch coast, but fared better than the *Association*, nor were they driven so far north, and after a few days in the North Sea they were back at home.

Ships all round the English coast from Milford Haven to Grimsby were battered by the storm, and havoc wrought among the ships in the Thames. Defoe describing the chaos on the river wrote:

> ...some vessels lay heeling off with the bow of another ship over her waste [waist], and the stem of another upon her forecastle, the boltsprits of some drove into the cabin windows of others; some lay with their stems tossed up so high that the tide flowed into their forecastles before they could come to rights; some lay so leaning upon others, that the undermost vessels would sink before the other could float.

Every catastrophe seems to bring at least one story of someone 'sleeping through it all', unaware that anything unusual was happening. Such an incident was recorded in 1703, when a waterman, slumbering in the cabin of his barge near Blackfriars, during possibly the worst storm in recorded history, was carried under the bridge and swept into Tower Dock, amid a tumult of debris and vessels out of control. He did not wake until the next day and learned with the greatest astonishment of the hurricane and his amazing survival. His words were not recorded; were they, perhaps 'Storm? What storm?'

Hurricane, 1987

The hurricane which struck England in the early hours of Thursday 15 October 1987, caught the country almost totally unawares; the weatherman during his 1.25 p.m. forecast the day before remarked 'Earlier on today, apparently, a woman rang the BBC and said that there was a hurricane on the way. Well, if you are watching, don't worry, there isn't!' In fairness it should be pointed out that the weatherman went on to say that there would be strong winds, and that there was a 'vicious-looking area of low pressure on our doorstep', but the forecast did not warn that probably the worst gale since 1839 was heading for this country. It later emerged that the Met. Office's emergency reports had not been issued to airlines, shipping and emergency services until just an hour before the hurricane struck. Why had the forecasters got it wrong?

One reason was the reduction in the number of weather-ships in the eastern Atlantic Ocean, there now being only three where at one time there were eight. Early in 1986 France withdrew its weather-ship from 'Point Romeo' 700 miles to the north-west of Finisterre, and no other European country stepped in to fill the gap. Most of Britain's weather comes from the direction of 'Point Lima' 500 miles west of the Clyde, but the hurricane came from the direction of 'Point Romeo'. The Met. Office was also hampered by an ageing computer, due to be replaced in a few weeks, and by a Civil Service strike in France, which prevented important meteorological information being passed on to Britain. Inevitably, however, there was general dissatisfaction with such explanations, many people feeling that it was a poor weather-forecasting service which failed to recognize an approaching hurricane. The newspapers next day reflected public anger with headlines such as 'Why weren't we warned?' (*Daily Mail*) and 'Met. Men fail to predict.' (*Daily Telegraph*). The Director General of the Met. Office firmly told the press, 'The Met. Office said there would not be a hurricane, and there was no hurricane', but while it was correct to say that the gale did not have the magnitude of a true West Indies hurricane, in several places the wind speed did meet the criteria for hurricane force, i.e. 77 m.p.h. for a duration of at least ten minutes. Such speeds were recorded at Gorleston in Norfolk (77 m.p.h.) and at Shoreham and Dover in Kent (85 m.p.h.)

Several people claimed to have known that a hurricane was on the way. It was noticed in west country ports such as Newlyn and Falmouth that boats from the French trawler fleet were coming in to take shelter on the evening before the gale; in the Falmouth harbourmaster's office one of the staff commented: 'It has to be pretty bad for the French to start coming in for shelter, maybe they know something we don't.' At Littlehampton in Sussex, Mr J. Ritchie alarmed at clouds scudding across the sky told his wife to bring in any plants of which she was particularly fond from the greenhouse, and as it happened they spent much of the following day clearing up the remains of the greenhouse from the lawn. In the early hours of 15 October, just before the gale struck, the cadet sailing-ship, *Royalist*, crewed mainly by teenagers, was passing Portland Bill on her way to Poole. David Norman, second-in-command of the ship, later commented:

> The master and I were not satisfied with what the forecasts were saying. Both of us are foreign-going master mariners and we did our own forecasting ... we decided that with such a very young and

inexperienced crew the most prudent action was to scuttle into
Weymouth. We got there – and we didn't regret it!

At Bungay in Suffolk a man who had repaired a barometer took a
last look at it before going to bed, and like Daniel Defoe, 280
years earlier, concluded that the instrument was not working
properly because the reading was so low.

With morning light the scale of the disaster became apparent.
People all over the south of England emerged from their houses,
just as they had done after the storm of 1703, to view the
devastation and take stock of the damage. It was phenomenal:
chimneys had crashed through roofs; trees lay across cars; power
and telephone lines had been torn down; lorries had been blown
over; walls flattened and streets full of debris of every description.
Some three million households and businesses were without
electricity and at least 400,000 were still without power three days
later. 150,000 telephones had been cut off and half were still not
reconnected a week later. Many villages and towns were
completely cut off by road due to fallen trees. Ninety per cent of
Kent's roads were blocked and part of the M4 motorway was
impassable, making it extremely difficult to reach London by car
from the west. No trains were running at all on British Rail's
Southern Region where 5,000 trees had fallen on the lines, while in
the Eastern Region it was two days before trains serving East
Anglia could leave from Liverpool Street Station, 2,000 trees
having to be shifted from the tracks. It is thought that insurance
claims for the night's damage amounted to £1,000 million.

Nineteen people were killed that night, or died later from
injuries, a surprisingly low figure when one considers the
enormous number of falling trees, walls and chimney-stacks.

Perhaps one of the most poignant deaths was that of Terence
Lee Marison, who was killed when the ancient plane tree under
which he was sleeping in Lincoln's Inn Fields, blew down, striking
him on the head. All that seems to be known of him was that he
was sixty-five years old and was born in County Durham. No next
of kin could be traced and he was buried by the council.

With happier endings were stories of babies born during the
hurricane. At Bexhill-on-Sea, police and ambulance men failed in
desperate attempts to reach a woman in labour and needing
hospital attention. Unable to get a vehicle to the house, they
eventually carried her through the storm on a stretcher, by way of
a hole in a garden fence and across a neighbouring garden, to
reach an ambulance. The baby was safely born in the hospital, but

only after a consultant had had to abandon his car on the blocked roads and make an hour's journey on foot through the hurricane.

At a village near Haywards Heath in Surrey, CB radio was used to call up a local midwife, and the baby was safely delivered at home – amidst a houseful of people who had also arrived to help. The mother later recalled:

> The baby arrived at 10.45 a.m. Literally five minutes after he was born, an ambulance, a fire engine, a tender in case it broke down, and a breakdown vehicle too, all arrived outside. Suddenly there were 14 people in my bedroom – ambulance men, policemen, friends ... all glad and all of them congratulating us ... I know that day was a dark one for many other people, but for us it was a happy one.

That night one of the few remaining English windmills in working order nearly met its end by fire; it was one of a pair, known as Jack and Jill, which stand on the top of the South Downs in Sussex. They represent the two basic designs of windmill, the tower mill and the post mill, and this is the only location in Britain where the two types can be found together. Jack, the tower mill, has a revolving cap on top of its brick tower, equipped with a fantail which keeps it, and the attached sails, facing into the wind. Jill, the post mill, is largely constructed of wood, and its entire superstructure, forty-three feet tall, and weighing three tons, revolves to face the wind. The internal mechanism of Jack had been missing for years, but Jill, after thirteen years of work by a preservation society, had been restored to working order. On the night of the hurricane Robert and Vera Deering, whose house is situated between the mills, were awakened by the wind, and when Bob Deering looked out of the window he saw sparks streaming towards him from the direction of the post mill. 'Jill's on fire!' he shouted, and immediately telephoned Simon Potter, a member of the preservation group who lived in Clayton Village. Mr Potter recalled:

> I grabbed a torch, pulled on the first clothes I could reach and 'phoned two other members who live nearby. The lane was blocked by trees in both directions, so there was no hope of using the car. The only thing was to walk, and I set off up the hill. It was so dark that I could only see 30 yards ahead. I had no chance of finding the path – I just went upwards. I knew the mills were above me, but I couldn't see them.

He was blown completely off his feet several times, and halfway up the hill saw one of the blades from Jill's fantail lying in the grass. The blade, which weighed about a hundredweight, had been carried for a distance of about 200 yards. At the top of the hill it was almost impossible to stand upright, and he crawled the last fifty yards on his hands and knees. The noise was deafening as he fought his way up the steps, and climbed into the mill's interior. It was pitch-black, full of smoke, and swaying like a ship in a gale. The sweeps were turning, despite the brake being on, and the smoke was caused by the friction between the brake wheel and the brake shoe. Mr Potter released the brake and the sweeps began to turn freely, soon reaching a speed, he thought, of between thirty and thirty-five revolutions per minute. This could quickly have shaken the mill to pieces – normally the sweeps only turn at about fifteen times a minute – so the brake had to be reapplied with extra friction to prevent slipping. The usual way of doing this was to apply ashes to the brake mechanism, so this was done, and the brake lever reapplied; but the friction was still not great enough to make the brake hold, so Mr Potter, who had now been joined by Bob Deering, rushed outside to scoop up buckets of gravel. Several friends were now making their way up the hill, but then a glow was seen at the top of the mill. Sparks had set it on fire.

A human chain was quickly formed and buckets of water passed from hand to hand from the house, about forty yards away. Finally, after two hours work, the weary men managed to stop the sails and bring the fire under control. As dawn came stock was taken. Sparks from the brake wheel had left a line of deep burns in the floorboards, and most of the three-inch wooden rim of the wheel, which was about six feet across, had been burnt away. When the mill had been blown backwards it had jammed and could no longer turn to face the wind. Until the structure could be repaired wire stays would have to be fitted to stop the mill falling over if a strong wind blew from any other direction. It was thought that about £5,000 worth of damage had been caused, and that the repairs would take as long as eighteen months. However, the mill had survived.

It was estimated that some 15 million trees were blown down in the hurricane of 1987, perhaps the most famous casualties being the oaks at Sevenoaks in Kent. In fact, there were two lines of oaks, the first seven having been planted in 1902 to mark the coronation of Edward VII, and the second seven after World War II, a gift from Canadian airmen who had been stationed nearby. Six of the first group and three of the second were blown down. It was trees such as these, carefully planted and nurtured over the years, and now a familiar part of the landscape, rather than those out in the country, which were perhaps most sorely missed.

Parks, estates and public gardens suffered greatly. The pleasure ground at Petworth in Sussex, and its surrounding great park, created by Capability Brown in the 1750s, was almost unrecognizable after the storm. The very trees planted by Lancelot Brown, grown to enormous size, were thrown down, including a splendid Lebanese Cedar and the largest sweet chestnut ever recorded in Britain. At the National Trust property of Scotney Castle in Kent, Mick Martin, the head gardener, said: 'When I got up the next morning and found that the drive was completely buried in trees, so that you couldn't even see where it went – I literally packed up. Absolute despair, that was the first sensation.' The garden lost 183 of its 531 trees. One of the oldest lime trees in Britain, planted 293 years ago, with a girth of 19 feet and 110 feet high, was blown down, as was a 171-year-old chequer tree or sorbus, once common in ancient woodlands but now rare.

At the Royal Botanical Gardens at Kew, where some five hundred trees were blown down and at least another five hundred badly damaged, Alan Beyer, the deputy curator, told *The Times*, 'This is the worst day in the entire history of Kew. It is impossible to put any kind of financial valuation on the damage.' It was thought it could be as long as a hundred years before the gardens looked anything like their pre-hurricane condition. Some of the trees were virtually irreplaceable, such as the Iranian elm planted in 1761, and a sweet chestnut which was thought to be 300 years old and a relic of the woods that grew on the site before Princess Augusta began to construct the gardens there in 1759. A carved mural was made from wood gathered from the fallen trees, in an attempt to produce something lasting and positive from the devastation. It was designed by Terry Thomas and carved by Robert H. Games, who selected between thirty and forty different types of wood, exploiting the colours and textures to suit the design and concept. Robert Games described to me how the idea evolved:

> A design was needed to portray the speed and strength of the wind. Ideas of devils and gods of wind moved on to that of a running man, leaving a trail of devastation behind him. During the storm a Turkey Oak planted by Princess Augusta at the founding of the gardens, crashed to the ground just short of the two stone lions beside the lake. Twigs and branches engulfed them and they suffered no damage at all. Here lay the central feature for the mural

– the confrontation between the 'storm man' and the two animated lions in defence of the tranquil gardens ... The inclusion of fleeing resident animals completes the picture.

Several naturalists were quick to point out that the gale was not an unmitigated disaster for the countryside. Gales with the intensity of the 1987 hurricane probably occur about every three hundred years, they said, a comparatively frequent occurrence in the lives of many woodland trees, and they should be looked upon as part of the natural cycle. The large clearings which had been created in wooded areas would now slowly fill up with a variety of vegetation, herbs, flowering plants, shrubs and young trees, which would benefit many species of animals and birds. The decaying wood would also benefit wildlife, innumerable species of insects thriving in fallen trees, in turn providing food for birds and animals – there should be no hurried replanting with just the obvious native species.

Many people have described the strange euphoria which was felt in southern England during the days following the storm, and the reasons for this are not hard to find; the clearing-up operations brought a brief period of excitement and outdoor activity to many folk unable for a brief spell to make the daily journeys on commuter trains; there was a feeling of shared hardship, inevitably likened by the press to that accompanying the blitz. People became 'good neighbours' seeking out and taking supplies to those who needed help, for with the failure of the basic services and loss of amenities the only recourse was to human effort and goodwill.

Hurricane, 1990
At 8.05 a.m. on Wednesday 24 January, 1990, Jack McGinnigle, the chief forecaster at the Meteorological Office at Bracknell, Berkshire, watched a three-inch-wide spiral of cloud moving across his computer screen. The spiral represented a gigantic cyclonic depression, perhaps the size of Spain, moving across the Atlantic Ocean towards the British Isles at 100 m.p.h. This was the hurricane of 1990. Unlike the storm of 1987 it did not take the weathermen by surprise, and as early as the previous Sunday they had predicted high winds, after monitoring the formation of a depression off Nova Scotia as cold air mixed with warm winds moving north from the Gulf Stream. Unusually, the storm grew in ferocity as it approached Great Britain. Brian Hoskins, professor of Meteorology at Reading University, commented, 'This was a fresh, adolescent storm that grew explosively in the final stage of

its route to Britain. Normally the storms we get are OAPs that have exhausted themselves on the way over.' The depression was photographed by the Meteosat satellite orbiting the earth's equator, which transmitted pictures through a ground station in Hampshire to the Met. Office computer screens. At 6.30 p.m. on Wednesday, the Met. Office contacted the Ministry of Defence to say that military help might be needed with the extensive structural damage that would be caused by the gales, and fifteen minutes later a national warning was broadcast. The warning was repeated on the BBC's 9 p.m. television forecast, and at 4 a.m. on Thursday a crisis message was issued to the country's emergency services.

The hurricane struck the tip of Cornwall at 6 a.m. that morning, waking up Peter Horder, a gardener at Trengwainton Gardens in Penzance. He opened the door of his cottage to see trees which had survived the storm of 1987, and indeed the gales of the past 150 years, being torn down by the wind, which was later thought to be in excess of 100 m.p.h. 'As I watched, the skies grew greyer and greyer, the wind more fierce,' he afterwards recalled, 'It was heartbreaking to see the damage and be powerless to help ... I was close to tears. The wind was howling and screaming and wreaking havoc.' When the wind finally abated, some three hours later, Mr Horder, who had worked at the National Trust gardens for twenty years, took stock and found that a third of the estate's trees had been destroyed.

The gale moved on. At Launceston, Stephen Blake, a thirty-year-old poultry-farmer, had just finished feeding his chickens when a sudden gust of wind lifted a complete 120-foot-long chicken-house and threw it three hundred yards. A few minutes later the remaining three chicken-houses collapsed, killing 10,000 birds. 'This is ten years of my life down the drain', commented Mr Blake. At Cullompton in Devon, Ian Cummings, a 55-year-old market-gardener, watched from his kitchen window as his greenhouses were blown up into the air, like enormous plastic bags, before exploding. A third of his crop – tomato plants and chrysanthemums – was destroyed Mr Cummings said:

> It started at around 8.15 a.m. with two or three dramatic gusts of wind. Then it calmed down until noon. Then suddenly glass was flying everywhere. When we walked back to pick up the wreckage the radios that had been left in the greenhouses were still playing. It all happened so fast.

The storm swept on across the country bringing the same sort of devastation that had occurred in the gale of 1987: roads and railways blocked by fallen trees; widespread structural damage; disruption of electricity supplies, and, inevitably, injury and death. At Swindon an eleven-year-old girl died in her classroom and other pupils were injured when the 100 m.p.h. wind tore the roof off Grange Junior School. Screaming children hid under desks as bricks and rubble showered on to them. The toll of injury might well have been higher had it not been for the prompt action of PC Adrian Wyse who was passing the school when he noticed the roof starting to lift. He rushed inside to warn the staff and the evacuation of the pupils was well underway when the hurricane struck the building.

A fifteen-year-old girl from Broxbourne, Hertfordshire, was killed by a falling tree as she left her school at nearby Ware, and a girl aged sixteen was killed at a school at Clevedon, Bristol, when a huge block of stone was sent crashing through the roof of the hall where the pupils were eating lunch. Five other girls were injured.

At Uppark House, a seventeenth-century mansion near Chichester, damaged by fire the previous year, the wind tore off part of the temporary corrugated iron roof and sent it hurtling into the gardens where it killed two workmen. 'We were absolutely devastated by the tragedy', said a National Trust spokesman. 'The south-west corner of the roof was torn away and carried about two hundred yards. Parts of it are still hanging over the house. Scaffolding around the house was also demolished.' Several other National Trust properties were damaged, or lost numerous trees, from as far apart as Castle Drogo in Cornwall, Belton House in Lincolnshire, and Erddig Hall at Wrexham in North Wales.

Several people were killed in their cars by falling trees, and Gordon Kaye, the well-known actor and star of the BBC television series *'Allo, 'Allo*, was injured while driving along Whitton Road, Hounslow, when part of a wooden hoarding crashed through the windscreen of his car. Ambulance men, on strike at the time, left their picket lines to help him (as they did with other emergency cases during the hurricane) and he was taken to hospital where he underwent brain surgery. He was very seriously injured, but slowly recovered and was seen on television again after a few months.

Roads throughout Britain were blocked by fallen trees, and there was great disruption to motorway traffic, the whole length of the M4 London–South Wales motorway being rendered impassable by overturned vehicles, with sixteen in the Thames Valley area alone. Fifty miles of the M5 between Taunton and Bristol were blocked, as were stretches of the M40 London–Oxford motorway,

and the M27 between Portsmouth and Southampton. Parts of the
M25 London orbital motorway were blocked and cleared several
times, as were stretches of the M1 between London and
Northants.

One-hundred-and-thirty people on board the Newhaven–
Dieppe Sealink ferry *Chartres* underwent a terrifying ordeal as the
vessel wallowed helplessly with her engines out of operation in
mountainous seas in mid-channel. She sent out an SOS call but the
rescue operation was called off when the crew managed to restart
the engines and take her into Dieppe.

This storm was in many ways more disastrous than that of 1987,
a greater area of the country was affected and more people were
killed, perhaps due to the fact that the hurricane struck in the
daytime when people were out and about. There was not the great
destruction of trees which had occurred in 1987, perhaps because
they had shed their leaves and offered less resistance to the wind.
It is thought that between three and five million trees were lost in
1990, compared with the fifteen million destroyed in 1987. The
most famous arboreal casualty of the 1990 hurricane was the
Selborne Yew; this massive yew tree, in the churchyard of St
Mary's, Selborne, is perhaps 1,500 years old, and has survived the
worst gales ever recorded in the United Kingdom. It withstood the
storm of 1268, a 'violent wind', wrote the Cistercian monks of
Waverley Abbey 'which has plucked out the trees and dashed
buildings to the ground'; the gales which raged across England in
1658 and 1666; the Great Storm of 1703; and the hurricane of
1987; to fall victim to the fury of the wind in 1990. When the
famous amateur naturalist, the Reverend Gilbert White (1720–93),
curate of Selborne, measured the trunk of the tree he found it to
be 23 feet in circumference. It had added some eight inches by the
time William Cobbett (1763-1835) visited it in the summer of 1823,
and the present vicar of Selborne, the Reverend James Anderson,
recorded a girth of 26 feet, just beneath the part where the
branches grew out.

The vicar's wife, Phyllida Anderson, heard the tree crash to the
ground at about 3.00 p.m. on 25 January, later commenting: 'It
was pretty loud. I was looking out of the window and we were
looking to see what might come down and suddenly there was this
awful crack and that was it ... We felt rather like you do when a
monarch dies.' Her husband added: 'We would rather have lost
any other tree than that one ... It is a great tragedy for the village.
This tree has witnessed the church being built and has seen
generations come and go.'

Dr Francis Rose, a well known botanist who lived at nearby Liss, pointed out that the tree might regrow if it were quickly set back into its hole, and arboricultural lecturer John Whitehead, of the Merrit Wood College of Horticulture and Agriculture, who saw the tree's plight reported on television, decided to attempt the task. With the help of twelve of his first-year students the churchyard was cleared of debris, the yew pruned and then winched upright and set back into its hole. The tree is apparently still alive, but it could be as long as three years before it is known for certain that the replanting operation was a success.

A macabre feature of the episode was the discovery of human bones in the hole which the tree's roots had occupied. Altogether there seemed to have been seven or eight burials, with three complete skeletons being found, these belonging to two children aged six and twelve, and a teenager of about seventeen. A small piece of Roman pottery was also discovered. The bodies, which were probably buried before the tree was planted, may have been those of sacrificial victims. The bones were later reburied in the churchyard.

The hurricane of 1987 was followed by a period of relative calm, allowing recovery and repair, but there was to be no such respite after the storm of 1990, which was followed by a month of appalling weather, with frequent gales, sleet, snow and ice, and torrential rain which caused serious flooding in many parts of England. In Hereford and Worcester, the Wye was at its highest level for twenty years and flooded scores of homes and hundreds of acres of farmland. Flooding also occurred along the River Severn, and in the Thames Valley where, on 10 February, Thames Water vans toured the streets warning people to boil their drinking water, after the flood contaminated water supplies to 32,000 homes. Then, on 26 February, following these four weeks of misery and chaos, there were further disastrous gales which caused eighteen deaths, widespread structural damage and breaches of the sea defences all round the coast. In Kent there was serious flooding at Folkestone, Hythe, Dymchurch and St Mary's Bay, while on the north Devon coast the wind-augmented high tide brought chaos at Appledore, Bideford, Ilfracombe and Lynmouth. In Sussex there was flooding at Elmer, Eastbourne, Shoreham, Worthing and Chichester. In the north-west, Lancaster, Morecambe and Fleetwood were flooded, as was New Brighton on the north Wirral coast.

The most disastrous coastal flooding, however, occurred at Towyn and Kinmel Bay on the North Wales coast, where a thousand people had to be evacuated from their homes. The catastrophe was similar to that which had occurred on the east coast thirty-seven years earlier, though happily no lives were lost. There were, though, all the other wretched features of the 1953 flood: frantic evacuations, homes ruined by sewage-contaminated floodwater, the loss of treasured personal mementoes.

The Government gave £150,000 to Towyn and promised to meet 85 per cent of the council's relief bill. There was, however, little help to people whose possessions were not insured, but a Mayor's Fund was set up to try to help those most in need. The *Guardian* of 29 August 1990, reported that six months after the inundation at Towyn, 700 people were still homeless, and that doctors were treating many patients with stress-related illnesses.

Mr Stork's wrecked cottage. The arrow indicates the height at which the 1657 flood stone was mounted

Channels gouged in the side of Round Hill by columns of water which struck Langtoft during the deluge

Wrecked bungalow at South Beach, Hunstanton, after the floods in 1953

Mrs P.K. Carr standing alongside a neighbour's uprooted chalet in Jaywick, 1953

Albert Street, Harwich, scene of the rescue of Mrs Yvonne Roberts, then aged fourteen

The camera caught the moment of collapse of this cooling-tower at Ferrybridge power-station during a gale in November 1965

Scots pines were uprooted at Birkenhead by hurricane force winds in 1987

Heatwave, August 1990. Bewl reservoir, near Lamberhurst, Kent, was stricken by the drought. *Inset*: This lucky pig cools off in a water-trough at Hall Farm, Norfolk

8   Tornadoes and Waterspouts

To many of us the word tornado probably brings to mind images of dark, sinister, funnel clouds sweeping across the plains of middle America; or perhaps the picture of Dorothy's house being swirled up into the clouds in *The Wizard of Oz*. Tornadoes, sometimes known in the USA as 'twisters', seem such a distinctive part of American culture that it is surprising to learn, according to Dr. G.T. Meaden who founded the Tornado and Storm Research Organization in 1974, that the country which experiences most tornadoes in relation to its size is Great Britain. British tornadoes, or whirlwinds, however, are not as large and destructive as their American counterparts, but have at times brought death and destruction.

Tornadoes have been the subject of a considerable amount of research, but their precise cause is still not entirely established. Generally speaking they seem to occur as a result of convection, with the rising of warm air and the falling of cool air, most commonly forming in association with thunderstorms at the point where advancing masses of cold dry air meet, overrun and displace masses of warm, moist air. The ascending air turns as it rises due to the variation of wind force with height and the proximity of a downdraught of cold, dry air. The strong updraught thus acquires a rotary movement which gradually extends along its length, increasing the speed of rotation as its diameter decreases. Just as water runs more quickly from a bath by spiralling down the plug-hole, so the ascending moist air is carried upwards more efficiently when following a similar spiralling movement. As the spinning air column lengthens beneath the clouds, it becomes visible when water vapour condenses within it, and if the rotary movement is strong enough the base of the funnel cloud will reach the ground.

The foregoing is only the most basic outline of the tornado process, the finer details being the subject of much debate among meteorologists. At one time it was widely thought that electricity

137

was a primary cause of tornadoes, but this idea has largely fallen out of favour in recent years. Nevertheless, tornadoes are usually accompanied by extremely violent electrical storms, and some very curious phenomena, which support the electrical hypothesis, have been reported in association with them. These include strange lights, ball lightning, evidence of burning along tornado tracks and sulphurous smells. Furthermore, according to R.T. Ryan and B. Vonnegut, miniature tornado-like vortices have been produced in the laboratory by high-voltage electrical discharges.

Typically a tornado appears as a writhing grey column (the colour is a result of the water vapour within it) perhaps a mile high and often likened by witnesses to an enormous elephant's trunk. Sometimes the colour changes according to the dust and debris sucked up, while the axis may be straight, contorted, vertical or inclined towards the horizontal. Tornadoes generally move across the country in a straight line, though they may sway from side to side and their course is often affected by various topographical features, a zigzag movement, for example, sometimes being reported. They often move with a 'hopping' motion, the base of the funnel cloud reaching the ground one minute and then lifting up the next. They may travel at between 5 and 65 m.p.h. though an average speed would perhaps be between 20 and 30 m.p.h.

Tornadoes are often accompanied by a shrill whistling noise, this changing to a deafening, roaring crescendo as they strike, the noise often being sufficient to drown out the sounds of the general commotion of falling buildings and other destruction. Electrical storms, as already mentioned, often precede or accompany tornadoes, and there are falls of gigantic hailstones on occasion.

For obvious reasons it is difficult to measure the wind speed generated in tornadoes, but it has been calculated that it may reach 325 m.p.h. In some British tornadoes it is estimated that speeds of 250 m.p.h. have been attained, and G.T. Meaden has suggested that nuclear power-stations should be built to withstand such blasts; at present they are constructed to withstand wind speeds of 150 m.p.h. When one considers that on one day, 23 November 1981, 102 tornadoes were recorded in Britain, and that on 19 January 1962, a violent tornado struck Egremont in Cumbria, just five miles from Sellafield the threat is not so unlikely as it might first appear.

Tornadoes are usually preceded by exceptionally heavy, sultry weather and high humidity. Dark heavy clouds swirl overhead, rolling over and over and into each other until a funnel cloud is formed, witnesses sometimes commenting that the day became as black as night before the column appeared. In some cases many writhing vortices are seen in the clouds and several tornadoes may descend from these.

Damage by tornadoes is caused in four different ways:

By direct impact. In mathematical terms, wind force is proportional to the square of wind speed, so that a rotary, tornadic wind of 300 m.p.h. exerts a force not ten times but *100 times* greater than one of 30 m.p.h., and a 300 m.p.h. wind may produce a pressure of 200 lbs or more per square inch.

By twist. When a narrow tornado passes over a tree the wind speed on one side of the tree may be much greater than that on the other, so the tree top is simply twisted off. Large mature trees may be destroyed in this manner.

By explosion due to reduced air pressure. It is known that a tremendous reduction of air pressure occurs within the vortex of a tornado. Normal air pressure is 14.7 lbs per square inch, but it has been estimated that it might fall to as low as 4 lbs per square inch within a tornado. As a tornado approaches a building, the great inequality between air pressure inside the funnel and that on the outside may blow the building apart.

By uplift. The updraughts within a tornado may reach speeds of over 200 m.p.h. and these are obviously capable of great feats of levitation. Trees are torn out by the roots and hurled high into the air, as are the roofs of buildings, cars, farm animals, people and objects of every description. Often these simply crash to the ground again, but sometimes in this bizarre phenomenon they are lowered gently on the outer rim of the tornado where upcurrents are just below what is needed to keep them aloft. There are reports of the most delicate objects being whirled aloft and set down safely in this way.

In recent years meteorologists such as M. Rowe and G.T. Meaden have discovered in early sources many accounts of British tornadoes, though as one might expect they are often described in a confused, exaggerated and superstitious way, sometimes being regarded as visitations of the devil. There are references to events which might have been tornadoes as far back as the eighth and ninth centuries, such as the one in the *Annals of Ulster* which describes 'a great and most mighty wind' accompanied by thunder and lightning which destroyed the monastery at Cluain Bronaig. However, the earliest indisputable reference to a tornado seems to be in the *Chronicon Scotorum*:

> In the year of Our Lord 1055, on Sunday the feast day of St George, the people of Rosdalla, near Kilbeggan in the present county of Westmeath, saw standing high up in the air, a great steeple of fire, in the exact shape of a circular belfry, or what we now call a round tower. For nine hours it remained there in sight of all: and during the whole time, flocks of large dark-coloured birds without number kept flying in and out through the door and windows. There was among them one great jet-black bird of vast size ...
>
> Sometimes a number of them would swoop suddenly down, and snatch up in their talons dogs, cats or any other small animal that happened to lie in their way; and when they had risen again to a great height they would drop them dead to the ground.
>
> At last they flew away towards a neighbouring wood; and the moment they left the tower it faded gradually from the peoples' view. The birds perched on the trees, the great bird choosing a large oak for himself; and so great were their numbers that the branches bent to the ground under their weight. There they remained for some time as if to rest; when suddenly they all rose into the air; and when the great bird was rising he tore the oak tree by the roots from the earth, and carried it off in his talons.

(A description of this incident appears in *The Wonders of Ireland* by the Irish writer P.W. Joyce, 1827–1914, apparently being a compilation of accounts from sources such as the *Chronicon Scotorum*.)

At least four features in the above account mark out the event as a tornado: firstly there is the reference to the fiery tower, this is probably intended to convey the movement of smoke in a large fire. Several witnesses of tornadoes in modern times have likened their appearance to pillars of fire and smoke: writing of a tornado in Buckinghamshire in 1950 (described later in this chapter) L.C.W. Bonacina comments: 'those who saw the vortex at close quarters likened its appearance to that of a fire, because of the dense masses of dust which were whirled aloft.'

Secondly, there is the reference to birds flying in and out of the tower; these undoubtedly are pieces of debris carried up by the tornado. Again, several witnesses in modern times have likened flying debris to birds; for example, a Mrs P.L. Flanagan who experienced the Birmingham tornado of 1931 saw what she first thought were birds flying past a window, then realized they were roof tiles.

Thirdly, there is the reference to animals being snatched up and then dropped to the ground; and finally the tearing up of the oak as the tornado departed, features highly characteristic of tornadoes.

Like other meteorological phenomena, tornadoes were widely regarded in a very superstitious light until well into the seventeenth century, but with the spread of scientific knowledge they came to be described in a more prosaic manner. The following account is of a tornado in Cheshire in 1662 (the year in which the Royal Society was incorporated). It occurred on 20 July, a day marked in Cheshire and Lancashire by violent thunderstorms and falls of enormous hailstones. It was described in *Admirable Curiosities*, published in London in 1682:

In the same day, in the afternoon, in the forest of Maxfield [Macclesfield] there arose a great pillar of smoke, in height like a steeple, and judged twenty yards broad, which making a most hideous noise, went along the ground six or seven miles, levelling all the way: it threw down fences and stone walls, and carried the stones a great distance from their places, but happening upon moorish ground not inhabited, it did the less hurt. The terrible noise it made so frightened the cattle, that they ran away, and were thereby preserved; it passed over a cornfield, and laid it as low with the ground as if it had been trodden down by feet; it went through a wood, and turned up above an hundred trees by the roots; coming into a field full of cocks of hay ready to be carried in, it swept all away so that scarce a handful of it could afterwards be found, only it left a great tree in the middle of the field, which it had brought from some other place. From the forest of Maxfield, it went up by a town called Taxal and thence to Wailey Bridge [Whaley Bridge] where, and nowhere else, it overthrew an house or two, yet the people that were in them received not much hurt, but the timber was carried away nobody knew whither. From thence it went up the hills into Derbyshire and so vanished. This account was given by Mr Hurst, minister of Taxal who had it from an eyewitness.

The Royal Society published several accounts of tornadoes in its *Philosophical Transactions*, such as the following concerning a whirlwind at Hatfield in Yorkshire on 25 August 1687, a hot, dry but cloudy day, with the wind:

...blooming out of several quarters at the same time ... the wind thus blowing soon created a great vortex, gyration and whirling amongst the clouds; the centre of which every now and then dropt down in the shape of a thick long black pipe, commonly called a spout, in which I could distinctly view a motion like that of a screw continually drawing upwards, and screwing up (as it were) whatever it touched ... coming to the place where I stood within 300 yards of me, I beheld this odd phenomenon, and found that it proceeded from nothing but a gyration of the clouds by contrary winds meeting in a point of centre.

In his account of the Great Storm of 1703, Daniel Defoe records that it was preceded by a tornado in Berkshire. The whirlwind was seen at about four o'clock in the afternoon of Friday 26 November 1703, one of the witnesses being the Reverend Joseph Ralton of Bessels Leigh who was called by a frightened countryman to go and see a 'pillar in the air' in a nearby field. The vicar later reported:

I went with the fellow and when I came found it to be a spout marching directly with the wind: and I can think of nothing I can compare it to be better than the trunk of an elephant, which it resembled, only much bigger. It was extended to a great length, and swept the ground as it went, leaving a mark behind. It crossed a field: and what was very strange (and which I should scarce have been induced to believe had I not myself seen it, besides several countrymen who were astonished at it) meeting with an oak that stood towards the middle of the field, snapped the body of it asunder. Afterwards, crossing the road, it sucked up the water that was in the cart-ruts; then coming to an old barn, it tumbled it down, and the thatch that was on the top was carried about by the wind, which was then very high, in great confusion.

The vicar did not follow the whirlwind any further but later heard that one of his parishoners was blown over and tumbled about by the tornado in a field about a quarter of a mile from Hinksey.

It was during the second half of the eighteenth century that the word 'tornado' first seems to have been used, though for a long time it was often applied to ordinary storms and gales. On the other hand, as late as 1775 tornadoes and whirlwinds were still sometimes referred to as hurricanes. The first correct use of the term seems to have been in the *Annual Register* for 1775 concerning a whirlwind at Stone, Worcester, on 21 August of that year, while in 1786 a correspondent to *The Gentleman's Magazine*, summing up the current thinking on tornadoes, commented:

That these phenomena depend upon electricity, cannot but appear very probable, from the nature of several of them: but the conjecture is made more probable from the following additional circumstances. They generally appear in months peculiarly subject to thunderstorms and are commonly preceded, accompanied, or followed, by lightning, rain or hail ... whitish or yellow flashes of light have sometimes been seen moving with prodigious swiftness about them.

Despite scientific scepticism in recent years concerning any major role played by electricity in tornado formation, it cannot be denied that what could be electrical phenomena have been reported in association with whirlwinds. In 1872, for example, a William Marshall who watched a tornado at Newbottle, Northamptonshire, saw a 'dark ball send up clouds of smoke and emitting red sparks', while during the south Wales tornado of 1913 there were reports of 'globular lightning'. Similarly, a Joseph Cameron, who saw a waterspout off the Needles in May 1944, reported that there was 'a bright red fire burning inside and throwing out quite big red sparks', and when the whirlwind struck Egremont in Cumbria in 1962, one witness, John Braithwaite, saw through a window a 'great ball of fire' coming straight towards the house.

A Whirlwind in Stanmore
Accounts of tornadoes became more detailed and scientific in the nineteenth century, a particularly clear description coming from a Colonel Beaufoy who, at about 12.30 p.m. on 26 April 1818, watched from Bushey, Hertfordshire as a whirlwind struck the neighbourhood of Stanmore. It had been a close, sultry, morning, and the colonel watched as the skies grew overcast and dense black clouds formed. Torrential rain quickly followed, accompanied by hail, lightning and thunder. After about half an hour the storm abated somewhat, and the colonel's attention was drawn to the clouds which 'appeared to roll over and over and into each other with considerable rapidity.' He continues:

Beneath these dark clouds there appeared a small white one, moving with surprising velocity towards the north-west; at the same time whirling round in a horizontal direction with prodigious quickness, accompanied with a horrid noise, which I can only compare to a stunning and most discordant whistle. The form of this white cloud was, in the first instance, that of a very obtuse cone with its apex downwards, which, during its rotary motion, occasionally approached and retired from the earth; the tail of the cone elongating continually as it receded, but on approaching the surface of the ground expanding like the lower part of an hour-glass, when it appeared to collect all the surrounding air into its immediate vortex, as it rebounded with such violence as to root up trees, unroof houses and hayricks, throw down walls and in short everything that impeded its progress.

The colonel described how the tornado seemed to have formed near a farm belonging to a Mrs Dickson, about a mile to the west of the village of Kenton in Middlesex. It travelled for a while in a north-westerly direction, but altered its course towards the north-east, then passed over Bushey village and through another farm and an orchard before finally breaking up about a mile and a half further on. The colonel describes in detail the damage caused by the tornado which seemed to grow in strength as it moved along. At Mrs Dickson's farm it removed ridge tiles and some of the thatch on outbuildings and hayricks. It then levelled the fruit trees in an orchard belonging to a Mrs Woodbridge, dashed a wooden outbuilding against her cottage and blew most of the tiles off the cottage roof. It then threw down eleven large elm trees in a field, the maximum width of the tornado being apparently no more than 100 yards at this point, trees to the left and right of this distance being undamaged. The tornado then crossed the Stanmore road and entered a nursery, badly damaging young trees; stripping away one side of the owner's house, blowing the thatch off hayricks and the roofs off the outhouses. Moving on to a nearby property it uprooted a large may bush, but curiously did not damage a greenhouse right next to it. It then passed through a plantation, again displaying a strange selectivity, for while one tree would be torn up by the roots, those around it would be untouched. As it approached the owner's cottage the tornado divided, leaving the building undamaged while throwing trees down on either side, and after passing the house the two parts united, tearing away wooden palings, stripping the tiles off outhouses and throwing down a large part of the garden wall. As the tornado reached the Marquis of Abercorn's estate it again seemed to divide, for it blew down two long lengths of garden wall, leaving a large section in between still standing. One of the Marquis's gardeners was blown to the ground and bowled over and over while he clutched at the grass to stop himself being carried any further. The tornado then crossed the road to the property of another neighbour, Mr Blackwell, tearing a field-gate from its hinges and tossing it into a ditch and also blowing down sixty-five feet of wall. It badly damaged several outhouses but left the house itself untouched. Colonel Beaufoy continues:

After leaving the garden it assailed a large beech, which measured at the base eight feet in circumference. My eye happened to be fixed on this tree at the moment; the wind commenced by giving its large head a considerable twist, and in an instant tore it up by the roots. After passing over the gravel pits at Harrow Weald, and a part of the village at Bushey, where it nearly unroofed a house, it continued its course without doing any further mischief until it reached Mr Bellas's farm. At this place its effects were very destructive among the fruit-trees and large elms, besides tearing away the tiles and thatch of the house, buildings and ricks; for here the storm appears to have contracted to a width of sixty yards, and its impetuosity to have increased in proportion as its breadth diminished. After passing in a north by east direction its fury most probably subsided ... The dreadful whistling noise continued unabated until the cessation of the storm.

The colonel added that as the tornado passed over the gravel pits it tore up the earth and gravel in patches, with intervals of undisturbed ground of 100 yards or more in between, the typical hopping pattern previously described. Also typical is the ear-splitting whistling noise; the curious selectivity of the tornado which damages objects in one place while sparing others immediately adjacent, and the proportionate increase in destructive power as the tornado narrows. The colonel goes on to say that he spoke to several people who had grabbed hold of hedges or fixed objects as the whirlwind struck, one of whom was Mr Blackwell mentioned above, who, returning from church with his son, clung to a post to save himself. Intriguingly, the colonel concludes by commenting that a meteoric stone may have fallen during the storm, for one of the Marquis of Abercorn's gardeners told him that he had seen 'a large stone about the size of his fist, descend in nearly a perpendicular direction, after a very dazzling flash of lightning, not followed by thunder.' They searched unsuccessfully for the stone and concluded that it might have fallen into a pond or been embedded in the soil, which was very disturbed at this spot. The colonel himself recalled a flash of lightning followed by a noise similar to the firing of a large rocket. There have been numerous accounts of stones hurtling out of the sky during storms, but scientists have always been sceptical of the phenomenon. These 'thunderstones' as they have been called are discussed in more detail in a later chapter.

The South Wales Tornado
Modern tornado investigation could be said to have begun with H.

Billett's *Geophysical Memoir* concerning the tornado of October 1913, one of the most violent British whirlwinds of this century. (It probably merits a rating of six on the TORRO scale.) H. Billett was a Professional Assistant in the Forecast Division of the Meteorological Office, and it was at the request of Clement Edwards, MP, that he spent three days collecting information in South Wales, where five people were killed and the worst structural damage occurred. His report ran to fifteen pages.

The tornado travelled from South Wales up to Cheshire during the late afternoon and evening of 27 October. Damage was intermittent, occurring along an eleven-mile track in the Taff Valley in Glamorganshire, continuing for twelve miles in Shropshire and for a further five miles in Cheshire. The thunderstorms which accompanied it had begun in South Devon, where the day had been fine and warm. At about 3.45 p.m. heavy clouds began to gather overhead and an extremely severe thunderstorm began, with torrential rain and terrific showers of hail; the storm moved northwards, across the Bristol Channel and into South Wales, the tornado apparently forming near Dyffryn Dowlais, to the north of Aberthaw. Here the track was some fifty yards wide, but little damage occurred until the whirlwind reached Treforest where the iron stack at the south end of the power-station was thrown down and the western side of the building, made of corrugated iron sheets, was blown outwards due to the reduction in air pressure. The force of the tornado had increased still further by the time it reached Cilfynydd, and the trail of destruction had widened to two hundred yards. The corrugated iron roof of a co-operative store was torn off and the sheets scattered, one later being found nearly a mile away and wrapped so tightly round a fallen telegraph pole that it could not be removed. A man was blown some thirty yards into a canal; the north side of the chapel was torn down; great damage was caused to roofs and interiors of houses in Richard Street and Wood Street and a number of hen-houses in allotment gardens were whirled upwards and never seen again!

The tornado continued northwards, killing a man near Abercynon, lifting him up and throwing him down again some fifty yards away. In Abercynon itself there was much structural damage, the roofs and joists of a row of thirteen houses being almost completely carried away. It seems to have been at its most violent at Edwardsville, where its trail was soon three hundred yards wide. Here a man was killed after being lifted up and carried for thirty yards and a small boy died when a wall was blown on to him. Again there was much damage to buildings and several slates were found afterwards buried to a depth of 1½ inches across the grain of trees. Mr B.P. Evans, headmaster of the Senior Boys' School at Treharris, described how the tornado struck his house in Edwardsville.

> A few seconds before 5.50 p.m. we heard a noise resembling the hissing of an express train. The sound grew rapidly in volume, at last resembling the rushing speed of many road lorries racing along. The oppressiveness that had been previously noticed increased, and the heat and air pressure were pronounced during the rushing noise.
>
> We endeavoured to move out of the room to the passage for greater safety, because a hurried remark was made that the engines of these, supposed, passing loaded steam-lorries had collided before the house, and were about to burst, when the panes of our window were broken by stones, tiles, slates, dried cement and splintered timber. The missiles broke the venetian blinds and struck the opposite walls. We made for the rear of the house, but all these windows were being bombarded also by small material and corrugated iron sheets. We could distinctly hear the chimney pots fall on the roof, and material sliding off being dashed on the pavement and doorstep.

The commotion lasted for between sixty and ninety seconds and was followed by torrential rain.

The tornado seems to have dissipated after striking Edwardsville, but it reformed near Church Stretton in Shropshire, causing great damage to trees and buildings over a 300–400 yard wide track which extended up to Shrewsbury. The trail again ceased, but began again at Wem and Whitchurch before once more disappearing, to reappear at Peckforton Moss in Cheshire where, like Colonel Beaufoy's tornado, it divided to pass a farmhouse, leaving it unharmed but destroying trees and buildings on either side. It then travelled along the foot of the Peckforton Hills, cutting a swathe a mile long and 150 yards wide through the woodlands, where the tops of many trees were twisted off, the distinctive characteristic of a tornado. Several cows were lifted over a high hedge into an adjacent field and three were killed, while pigsties, hen-houses and barns were demolished, some being lifted up and blown bodily away, wreckage and the dead bodies of animals being left strewn amongst the trees.

The tornado passed Beeston Castle, unroofing a farm on its eastern side; it caused much damage at Willington Hall, Kelsall, and eventually passed into Lancashire at Runcorn, where it seems finally to have dissipated. Curiously, only one person, Mr D.

Williams of Treharris, reported seeing the distinctive funnel cloud of the tornado, but its effects on trees, buildings and people were unmistakable. H. Billet comments that the width of the track, and the rate of advance (some 36 m.p.h.) were on a par with many American tornadoes.

As mentioned briefly on page 143 several witnesses reported ball lightning in connection with this tornado, one of these being Mr W.M. Morris of Cardiff who was travelling home from Pontypridd by train, and who later reported:

> Repeated flashes continued for four minutes, and the train travelled slower than usual, till we reached Creigiau Station at 5.23 p.m., when I clearly observed a ball of fire, apparently the size of my hat, flashing along with a blinding sheet of lightning, and travelling from south to north.

Four or five other people in the compartment verified his account, and ball lightning was also seen by Mr. T.A. Thomas of Pontypridd who stated:

> I saw nothing out of the ordinary run of thunderstorms until I had reached a point a little beyond Wood Street Schools. Here I observed a flash of lightning, which seemed to assume a globular shape, sending out a long tail-like stream of light.

Another five people at Cilfynydd reported a similar phenomenon.

Tornado, 1950
The longest known tornado track in the British Isles was formed on Sunday 21 May 1950. There were in fact three tornadoes involved, the main whirlwind originating in the area of the Chiltern Hills and first being seen in the Missenden-Wendover Valley just before 4.00 p.m. This tornado travelled for some sixty-five miles, causing £50,000 worth of damage before dying away near Feltwell in Norfolk. It then reformed some seven miles further on, ultimately travelling out to sea near Blakeney, giving a total track, including the break, of about 100 miles. Relatively little damage was caused by the subsidiary tornadoes, one of these being of only short duration and the other passing mainly over open countryside. Perhaps surprisingly, no one was killed by the actual tornadoes, though four people died, two as a result of lightning strikes, in the accompanying storms.

The damage caused by the main tornado began in the Missenden Valley around Little London and Smalldean farms, and was limited to a narrow trail until the whirlwind reached the point where the valley opens towards the Vale of Aylesbury when destruction on a larger scale commenced. Many fully grown trees, mainly elms and walnuts, were blown down and scattered in a trail fifty yards wide, in a meadow beside the London road near Wendover. The trail narrowed again as the tornado passed over Wendover, raising a column of water from the old canal and blowing the roofs off several of the older buildings. It then proceeded to the RAF camp at Halton, where it battered the trees and lifted the heavy roof of the power-station. The whirlwind was described by observers as resembling a giant palm tree with a broad base into which objects were sucked and passed up the main column, to be thrown out higher up, at heights of between 100 and 300 feet. The funnel cloud was seen to break up as it passed over an avenue of chestnut trees in its path, and a ground whorl, almost separated from the upper part of the column, continued over the next 300 yards.

The whirlwind went through seven or eight regenerations within forty minutes between Wendover and Leighton Buzzard, each marked by a sudden broadening, then narrowing, and temporary disappearance, of the trail on the ground. As it approached Aston Clinton, the column was seen to be about 200 feet clear of the ground, but it quickly descended, causing the usual damage to trees and buildings. Up to this point its path had been almost straight, but now it began to zigzag, possibly because of several closely grown coppices in its path. Still travelling along the ground, it left a narrow trail of severe damage at Aston Clinton, before rising up again, passing lightly over open ground to descend once more on farm buildings at Puttenham. Here the north-eastern end of a strongly built brick byre was thrown down and outwards; a large Dutch barn of six-inch iron girders was twisted up and bales of hay thrown out, and a nearby Nissen hut was destroyed, its floor being left impaled fifty feet up on the topmost branches of a tree.

At the Ascott Estate at Wing Ridge the whirlwind's course was very erratic: it threw down large trees, tore the branches off others and lifted vehicles in the farmyards. It then divided into three or four twisting columns, each of these causing its own path of destruction, before uniting to advance upon Linslade, on the outskirts of Leighton Buzzard. It was here that the damage was greatest (some £25,000 in all), most of the houses in Old Road and New Road having their roofs damaged or completely destroyed, the outhouses between the two streets being demolished. A brick-built bakery was demolished, telephone lines were torn down, and television aerials broken or twisted like corkscrews; a heavy roof near the railway station was blown off, and in the station yard a horse-box with its occupant was lifted and tossed about. The tornado rose above the ground several times in the Leighton Buzzard area, descending here and there to damage buildings, orchards and greenhouses. At Broom Hills farm two cows were killed, the whirlwind then proceeding to Shenley Hill nurseries, Heath, where apple and pear trees were uprooted and cold frames lifted up and carried over the greenhouses, to be set down undamaged! No further damage was caused for several miles but the twisting column was seen at several points and its passage accompanied by heavy rainfall, thunder and lightning.

The trail of destruction resumed at Harrowden Road on the southern edge of Bedford, where apple trees were uprooted, tiles blown off roofs and garden walls blown down. Several large trees were torn down at Fenlake, some being carried right over the River Ouse and others blocking the river itself, while willow trees along both banks of the river between Fenlake and Castle Mills Lock were felled. Only one or two people actually reported seeing the column at Bedford, it being obscured in the darkness caused by heavy thunderclouds, many people in Bedford remarking that it was the darkest day they had ever known. The tornado then seemed to weaken, there being little damage for the next fifteen miles, but as it reached St Ives, it gathered strength again: at Sutton, buildings were damaged, roofs lifted, the wall of a house blown out, an orchard uprooted and a ten-to-twenty yard swathe cut through a wood, mature oaks with trunks a yard thick being torn from the ground or twisted in two. The main road was blocked by trees and a bus-driver watched the tops of trees in front of his bus being torn off and blown towards him, before the bus itself was overturned.

The tornado diminished from this point, though there was some damage in the valley at Witcham and at Coveney. The cloud mass passed directly over the airfield at Feltwell, with dozens of twisting vortices at its base, but these did not descend lower than about 1,000 feet. The funnel cloud reformed, however, in the Shipdham area, and was last seen at Blakeney, Norfolk, before withdrawing into the clouds.

A lesser trail of damage was caused by a secondary tornado which seems to have originated in the Dunstable area at about 3.30 p.m. At Chapel End farm, near Houghton Conquest, it passed as a narrow column between two ancient barns, just nine feet apart, raising only a few ridge tiles from one of the barns but lifting a ten-to-fifteen-foot high waterspout from the pond which was between the two buildings; it then continued to Duck End Farm, Wilstead, where large trees were felled over a track some twenty yards wide and some £200–300 worth of damage caused, and next passed over open land, frightening animals and breaking down trees at Medbury Farm near Elstow. It passed the Bedford sewage pumping station, damaging houses, roofs and trees in the Goldington area, while frightened horses ran for safety at Putnoe Farm. The tornado then withdrew into the clouds, but it later regenerated, a swirling cloud being reported at Kimbolton, and damage to roofs and telephone lines was caused at Peterborough. As with the main tornado, this subsidiary whirlwind was accompanied by rain and storms and its path intersected the track of the principal tornado. Tornado 2 was causing damage at Wilstead while Tornado 1 was attacking Linslade.

A third tornado seems to have first been observed at Caldecote near Biggleswade at about 5.30 p.m. It lifted corrugated iron roofs, tore an eight-inch-thick branch off an apple tree, dropped it on to a car a few yards further on, and tore some tiles off the roof of the Methodist church. The trail of damage was less than a quarter of a mile long though, and nowhere more than five yards wide.

The tornadoes were accompanied by exceptionally severe thunderstorms, two people being killed by lightning and several others injured on open ground at Houghton Conquest. The lightning also disrupted electrical supplies, damaged buildings and killed several cattle. There were heavy falls of rain and hail, flooding being extensive in Bedfordshire, Northamptonshire, Buckinghamshire and the Fen country. The floods blocked several roads and on sloping ground the water removed top-soil and damaged crops. The heaviest rainfall occurred to the north and north-west of Bedford, one person being killed in a torrent of floodwater at Kimbolton. Showers of hail killed poultry, damaged crops and fruit trees, smashed greenhouses and broke windows. The largest hailstones fell at Ascott House near Linslade and at North Crawley near Newport Pagnell, these sometimes clumping together to form chunks of ice 6–6½ inches across and weighing about 4 ozs. In several places the roads were blocked by heavy drifts of hail: on the Bedford–Northampton road at Oakley it was eighteen inches deep, and at Turvey there were unconfirmed reports of drifts three feet deep.

Waterspouts
Waterspouts are formed over seas, lakes and rivers by

meteorological processes similar to those which generate tornadoes. A vortex of air descends from the clouds, the water beneath it beginning to churn and foam. As the funnel becomes lower, spray rises to meet it and the waterspout is formed. Around its base is a circular whirl of spray, or 'cascade', this being much wider than the spout itself. The funnel of a waterspout is largely condensed water vapour from the air, rather than a huge column of whirling water, but water can, nevertheless, be drawn up to a considerable height by the vortex; the water which formed the cascade of a waterspout off Massachusetts in 1896 reached a height of four hundred feet. Generally speaking the vortices which create waterspouts are not as violent as those which create tornadoes, for spouts are often formed in relatively calm weather, but there are exceptions and some of the larger, more violent spouts are true tornadoes, formed in association with thunderstorms over land and then moving out to sea.

Waterspouts are a bizarre phenomenon and appear in a variety of shapes and sizes. Most are simple columns, but some are hour-glass shape with the waist halfway between sea and sky. Spouts usually consist of a single column, but there are reliable reports of two, and even three, hollow concentric tubes, each rotating at a different velocity, a phenomenon which is far from being understood. Proportions vary considerably, some being a thousand feet tall but only twenty feet wide, while others may be two thousand feet high with a diameter of five hundred feet; they have been known to reach a height of five thousand feet but this is exceptional. Some meander across the water at 1–2 m.p.h. while others race along at 50 m.p.h. Waterspouts may last up to an hour, but most have a life of about twenty minutes. As well as appearing singly, they are often reported in twos and threes, and groups of up to fifteen have been recorded. They may form in a variety of weather conditions: in near calms and in gales; in warm and cold weather; in summer and winter and by day and night. Generally they are harmless but can be dangerous to small boats and aeroplanes.

Probably the earliest record of a British waterspout is in the *Flores Historiarum* compiled by the chronicler Roger of Wendover (died 1236) who reported that in June 1233, off the south coast of England, 'two huge snakes were seen by many along the coast, fiercely battling in the air, and after a long struggle one overcame the other and drove it into the depths.' Most accounts of waterspouts in the British Isles do indeed come from the south coast, and on Sunday 18 August 1974, there were numerous sightings in this area, extending from the Isle of Wight to Hastings.

For example, Mr K.L. Everard, skipper of the fishing boat *Southern Isle*, reported to the Shoreham coastguard that at 11.25 he had seen three waterspouts about five to six miles off Shoreham. He continued:

> At the time I was about 2 miles from the spouts. At my position the sea was mirror calm with no wind and thundery-type rain (large spots) and lightning in the black cloud. In the area of the waterspouts the cloud base was only 100 to 150 feet above the sea. At sea level, near the base of the spouts, there seemed to be a boiling mist and the sea appeared to be agitated around this area.

Another was seen by Mr. E.R. Gillam of Brighton who was fishing four miles west-south-west of Newhaven when, at 11.00 during rainy weather, the spout appeared about three miles to the south-west:

> It seemed very slow-moving and we looked at it for a while then hauled the trawl. After shooting the trawl I noticed the spout was moving very fast north-east, then Niton Radio gave out the warning on VHF informing all boats to keep clear. We thought the spout was going clear of us so we kept towing the trawl past. I put the radar on and watched for a while, when the spout changed course and started heading north-north-west which put it on collision course with my vessel. We then turned the boat round still towing the trawl (which takes some time) and by this time the spout was half a mile to the south-east of us where we had a close look at it. The disturbance on the water was terrific, brilliant white. It seemed to stay for a while then we moved away from it. We then heard a sand-dredger bound from Newhaven to the west calling up on the radio and saying the spout was collapsing.

Another witness was Mr G.J. Child of Hove in Sussex, who at the same time watched two waterspouts for about fifteen minutes. He estimated their height at about two hundred to three hundred feet, and said that they were very thick in relation to their height. The spouts were dark grey in colour, and slowly faded before growing clearer and then fading again, until they disappeared about fifteen to twenty minutes later. The weather was warm and overcast.

Mr J.R. Dale of Seaford, race official for the Newhaven and Seaford Sailing Club was organizing a race in Seaford Bay that morning, but was having great difficulty setting a course because the wind was continually changing direction. At about 11.15 the wind died away completely and shortly after Mr Dale saw a waterspout about four or five miles south-south-west of his office.

It appeared as a dark funnel with the wide upper part reaching the clouds, although the other end did not seem to touch the sea. The spout was watched carefully, and rescue craft kept close to the racing yachts. By 11.20 it was clear that the waterspout was travelling in a north-easterly direction towards the land, and it finally dispersed at about 11.45 when approximately 1½ miles offshore. Mr Dale commented:

> During the whole period mentioned above, the cloud formation was low-level scattered cumulus over the land and fairly continuous stratus over the sea. For the whole period of the waterspout, its top disappeared into the cloud base which was at a height I would estimate to be between 1,000 and 2,000 feet but probably nearer to the former. The only period which looked dangerous to yachts was between 11.20 and 11.25 when the sea surrounding the waterspout appeared to be very confused.

No less than six waterspouts were seen by Mr Grossmark of Brighton between 10.00 and 11.30 that morning as he was sailing between Gosport and Newhaven. They appeared during a thunderstorm and at one time were in a U-shape formation round the yacht at a distance of 2½–4 miles. The spouts lasted for between ten and twenty minutes before dissipating. Altogether there were at least eight reports of waterspouts that day.

A waterspout had been reported off the Devon coast the previous day; and a frightening encounter occurred at the end of the month, the principal witness being Mr B. Kenyon from Winchester who, in the early hours of Saturday morning, 31 August 1974, was in a yacht about five or six miles off Portland in Dorset. It had been a calm, clear night, Mr Kenyon distinctly remembered the display of stars over Lyme Bay, but the weather was changing. Rain came on, the sea grew rough, thunderclouds gathered and lightning began to strike over Portland and Weymouth. Mr Kenyon and his friend decided to make for Weymouth. The weather grew even worse as they came towards the Shambles light, and at 5.30 a.m. a great, grey column of water was seen to starboard, reminding them, said Mr Kenyon, of the whirlwind in *The Wizard of Oz*. The frightened observers dropped the foresail and secured it to the safety rails before lashing themselves into the cockpit. The rain was now very heavy, and the wind so strong as to make it almost impossible for them to keep their eyes open, but they could see that the waterspout was moving steadily closer. Mr Kenyon continues:

We were unable to guess what the waterspout would do or what direction it would take ... we were eventually able to see the shape and formation of the spout and it appeared, on recollection, to be anti-clockwise, water turbulent at the base. The water could be clearly seen rising into the column, the colour at the base was a muddy green-brown, though as you looked up the column it became more bluey-grey. Without an horizon it was difficult to give any indication of the height. From the detail that could be seen it was between 250 and 350 yards away passing us down the starboard side and astern. At the same time an extremely severe electric storm was lying around the boat and forked lightning striking the water. The width of the lightning was quite frightening, appearing to be a yard or more in width. We kept our hands away from all metal parts, said nothing to each other but were both rather shaken.

Miniature Vortices

Land-devils, or dust-devils, are rotary disturbances of the air similar to tornadoes but considerably less powerful. They are not part of large-scale air movements and electrical storms, like full-size tornadoes, but occur on fine, or hot days, when a warm, rising mass of air, perhaps heated by sun-baked ground, is suddenly overrun by a cooler mass of air, such as an advancing sea breeze.

Sometimes land-devils are completely invisible, detectable only by sudden bursts of wind accompanied by a hissing noise, but they may suck up dust, leaves, grass and litter and thus achieve temporary visibility. In desert regions land-devils may reach a height of 3,000 feet, and often form in groups which march along in formation, but it usually takes only the slightest disturbance of the rising warm air to cause them to collapse.

Water-devils are small-scale vortices which are seen over lakes and rivers. They often start as land-devils which then travel over water, but they may actually form over it and spray is then drawn up into the rotary wind.

These miniature vortices display surprising strength, a land-devil only two feet across being capable of lifting and scattering garden furniture. There seems to be no explanation at present as to how so much energy can be concentrated into such a small vortex.

A mini-tornado was reported in Hampshire in 1979. At 4 p.m. on 5 May, a group of players at Farnborough Tennis Club watched amazed as a whirlwind 25 feet high swept along for a distance of between 300 and 400 yards. One of the players commented:

We noticed a gust of wind first, which was not that unusual. Then we looked up and saw that papers and dust were being whirled up furiously ... one girl was a bit frightened and took a few steps away from it but the rest were more interested than worried. It disappeared about a hundred yards from us.

Another witness at the club was Peter Hutchinson, who added: 'We felt the terrific wind. It came towards us sucking up dust and rubbish into the air. It went past the tennis courts then disappeared on to the GLC estate.'

In other cases, people have reported rumbling noises or loud reports prior to the appearance of land-devils. For example, a group of picnickers at Pilsdon Pen in Dorset on 3 September 1955, heard about 1 p.m., a sound resembling a great load of sand being dumped into a truck. They then saw that the grass in the direction of the sound was moving and becoming flattened and bits of paper began to whirl around in the air. As the miniature whirlwind reached the picnic group it sucked a paper bag into the debris and an open umbrella was carried up to a height of twenty feet.

A similar incident at Launceston in Cornwall in 1918 attracted the attention of onlookers when a miniature whirlwind produced a noise like distant thunder and there is an account of a land-devil at Cupar in Scotland on 29 June 1842, which was preceded by a sudden, sharp, report. It is not known for certain what produces these sounds, but it has been suggested that these mini-vortices form high up in the atmosphere and that it is their sudden descent which produces the noise.

In the year 1886 on 27 August a land-devil was described near Portmore Lough on the eastern side of Lough Neagh in Northern Ireland. Two workers were standing in a recently mown meadow when they heard a rumbling noise like thunder, but sounding faint rather than far off. It was a fine warm day and completely calm without a leaf stirring and with only a few light clouds in the sky. Looking in the direction from which the sound had come, they watched as a whirlwind suddenly appeared about half a minute after they had heard the booming sound. They saw it whirl up a quantity of loose hay to a height of about a hundred feet; this floated in circles for a while then slowly descended, and on the ground a haycock was blown round. They said the whole episode was over in about a minute.

On 8 August, during the heatwave of 1990, a mini-tornado was seen by naturalist Chris Hall and his friend Robert Smith as they walked in the Fox Hills area, above Ash Common, in west Surrey. Fox Hills is a ridge about 360 feet high in a large tract of heathland, sandy and mainly covered by heathers with some scattered birch bushes. A huge heath fire had swept across this area two days previously and had left a surface covering of dust and ash. They first noticed the swirling column of black dust slightly below the top of the ridge and at first thought it was a dust-devil but soon realized it was much larger:

> ...it was lifting dust in a swirling cloud several feet high, moving erratically along the slope with an audible swishing sound. (We were about 300 feet away and lower down the slope.) When it engulfed a small birch bush the bush swayed wildly, as if in a gale.
>
> The cloud was broad at first, visibly swirling, several feet high (it looked at this distance to be taller than a man, say 7 to 8 feet), moving slowly NW to SE, then narrowed and seemed to be dissipating, as dust devils tend to do. But instead of fading out it funnelled into a point, like a miniature tornado, swirling still, a narrow funnel of dust spinning, and rising several feet. It was now closer to us, perhaps as near as 25-30 feet, and was moving only slowly.
>
> It moved a little away from us, into a saddle between the high ground of Fox Hills and a small hillock to the east, and seemed to become either stationary or rotating over a very localised spot only a few feet across. It maintained the narrow funnel shape, raising dust and ashes to a height of probably ten feet, and apparently gaining energy again. It maintained this semi-stationary condition for perhaps 20 seconds, then began moving again. It moved away from us, beyond the hillock and out of view. My last view was of a broadening cloud of dust above the hillock (the lower part of the funnel was out of sight at this stage).

They estimated the phenomenon was in view for about two to three minutes and thought it was so clearly visible because of the abundant dust and ash with which it coloured itself. Under normal conditions it would have been invisible, though not inaudible.

Loud reports have occasionally been mentioned in association with water-devils, as in the following case which occurred in Aberdeenshire, in June 1779. The witnesses were sitting by the side of a lake when:

> ...we saw a pillar of water rise as high as the tallest tree, and fall down again, after which it rolled along for a considerable space in large rolls as if a cask had been under the water, and out of those rolls sprung up small strings of water, rising pretty high, as out of the strop of a razor. The noise it made was such as a firework makes when first set off, but much louder. The day was clear, fine sunshine and not a breath of wind.

A detailed description of a water-devil was given by J. Gray in *Nature* in 1872. The incident occurred on 16 April of that year, on the river Elwys near St Asaph in North Wales, at a point about two miles above the Cefn caves. The witness reported that his attention was drawn to a strange hissing, bubbling sound as if a piece of hot metal had been plunged into water, and, on turning:

> I beheld what I may call a diminutive waterspout in the centre of the stream, some forty paces from where I was standing. Its base, as well as I could observe, was little more than two feet in diameter. The water curled up from the river in an unbroken cylindrical form to a height of about fifteen inches, rotating rapidly, then diverged as from a number of jets, being thrown off with considerable force to an additional elevation of six or seven feet, the spray falling all around as from an elaborately arranged fountain, covering a large area.

The water-devil remained in the same position for about forty seconds, then moved slowly in the direction of the right bank of the river before returning again towards the centre, where it remained stationary for a few seconds before moving towards the bank again. As it did so, it began to lose its force and finally collapsed. The witness pointed out that, curiously, the course of the spout was perpendicular to the bank and not following the direction of the current.

More violent than the water-devils so far described was one which appeared on Loch Dionaird in Sutherland in 1978 and which was reported in the *Sunday Post* for 12 February that year. Kenny Bell, from the Lodge Hotel at Old Rayne, Aberdeenshire, had organized an angling expedition to Loch Dionaird, but the fishermen had only been on the water for about half an hour when the wind blew up and they decided to return to shore. It was then that they heard a 'whooshing' noise and a spout of water ten feet high bore down on them. Before they could get out of the way, the boat was lifted out of the water and spun around, falling back on to the surface facing the opposite way. The anglers, soaked to the skin, watched terrified but fascinated as the spout whirled away across the loch before collapsing.

We have already seen how Roger of Wendover referred to the waterspouts as living creatures (see page 152), and Dr G.T. Meaden in an article in the *Journal of Meteorology* made the interesting and original suggestion that at least some reports of the Loch Ness Monster, particularly those from early times, could be explained by water-devils. It is easy to see how incidents such as the one on Loch Dionaird could be interpreted in more credulous times as encounters with demons or monsters.

9   Heatwaves and Droughts

In the British Isles the arrival of a heatwave is welcomed, especially after a series of dreary damp summers, but if the exceptionally hot days and nights continue for a prolonged period, the general feeling when the inevitable problems arise sometimes becomes 'enough is enough.'

Although the record temperature of 36.7°C (98.1°F) in 1911 was not exceeded in 1976, the heatwave persisted for almost the whole of the summer and the shortage of water soon became a very serious problem. For example, the normal flow over the Teddington weir in the Thames of 170 million gallons a day was reduced to 50 million, and many reservoirs, some feeding the conurbations, were less than half full while others were reduced to one tenth of their normal volume. By August there were many restrictions: in some areas supplies were cut off for up to seventeen hours a day, and there were wide-ranging prohibitions on the use of water for non-essential purposes, such as filling garden ponds and private swimming-pools, washing vehicles, cleaning buildings, and a total ban on the use of hosepipes.

Fire became an alarming hazard and there were a great number of woodland and heath fires raging in many areas, laying waste to many thousands of acres and destroying the wild life, particularly in the south of England. The *Farnham Herald* on Friday 9 July 1976 carried the headline 'Firemen stretched to breaking point', borne out by Mr Chris Hall of Fleet in Hampshire who noted:

June 30. Smoke around all day. I set out to find what was happening ... drove towards Ash ranges, then saw a second smoke cloud in direction of Frensham, and decided my help would be more valuable on the National Trust land. In fact it was in the Elstead/Thursley area. The fire was huge. Roads were closed; the village of Thursley was threatened. The fire had been raging since 2 p.m. yesterday, making 28 hours when I left, with no sign of the end. Bulldozers were on the heath creating firebreaks. The situation was hopeless. As I drove back to Fleet there was smoke everywhere, something like eight separate columns. The Thursley fire had split into three, raging across different parts of the common, two fires on Ash ranges, two from the Deepcut direction and one from Hook Common.

1 July. Fires still raging. There has been a continuous area of smoke from Ash Common, and other blazes on Yateley Common and Blackbushe. The railway had to be closed near Fleet yesterday due to thick smoke over the lines. The scale of this is even leaving the destruction of last spring in the shadows.

Another problem, sinister and not immediately evident, was the subsidence of property built on a clay base, and insurance companies were called upon to meet a record number of claims. During a long dry spell, the clay shrinks, causing house foundations to distort and the buildings to crack and tilt.

Perhaps what really distinguished the heatwave in the minds of many people were the ladybirds. 1976 was the 'Ladybird Summer', when these normally benign little creatures, loved by children and gardeners, suddenly became menacing by their sheer numbers. The majority were of the two-spot variety, these far outnumbering the seven-spot and fourteen-spot. A correspondent, Mrs Joyce Bennett, described a family outing which turned into a nightmare:

I was driving from Wrexham to Rhyl with my children, my mother and niece on a lovely sunny day, when my boys in the back suddenly began to argue over a ladybird, which had arrived through an open window. Driving along, the commotion in the back began to get out of hand, and I was told that there were now a large number of ladybirds in the car.

I then noticed that large numbers of them were on the windscreen, both inside and out. I drove about 300 yards and had to pull into the side of the road, and when I got out of the car I noticed large black clouds of them around and over my car. Everyone got out and we were covered from head to toe with millions of ladybirds. Meanwhile other motorists were pulling up ... We spent half an hour trying to get rid of them and then returned to the car and beat a hasty retreat.

They reached Rhyl and there they found, despite the sunshine and the large number of cars containing families, there was no one on the beach. The children were delighted, no crowds and the tide almost in!

They undressed and ran from the car, only to return again covered from head to foot with ladybirds. They were *frantic* and we had to swat the things away and all pile back into the car. Then it rained:

we watched these clouds of black insects for about three hours. Then they disappeared, and we again ventured from the car. All around us, about 4–5 inches deep, were dead bodies of ladybirds. It was quite eerie, and we had no idea of what had actually happened until we read about them in the paper the next day.

The *Sunday Times* of 31 December 1989 carried the headline, 'Britain enjoys warmest year since 1659 – Official.' For the first time since 1900 the Met. Office classified all four seasons of one year as 'Very warm', and the 'Greenhouse effect' now became almost a household expression. In 1989 the newspapers again carried pictures of drying-out reservoirs and people visiting villages which were reappearing, deserted, in long-submerged valleys. A correspondent wrote to me in August 1989:

...we visited the Fenworthy reservoir which serves Torquay. Because of the lack of rain the water had dropped considerably and we were able to walk right round it, on the outer edges of the dried-up bed of the reservoir. We spotted a man fishing in the reservoir and discovered that he was standing on what used to be a bridge over the original river that flowed there before the dam was built before the war. What at first looked like two boats from the distance, proved to be the original walls on either side of the bridge. Normally this would be many feet below the surface. Because he was standing *on* the original bridge he was only up to his knees in water but with deeper water around him.

The full facts and figures for the heatwaves of 1990 are not yet known, but the *Times*, as early in the year as 29 April, announced that the season's first hosepipe ban was to be imposed:

The season's first hosepipe ban signalled the onset of summer this weekend, as Britons sunbathed in temperatures as hot as those in south Spain. Temperatures peaked in London at 64 F (18 C) hotter than Rome and the same as Marbella, Lisbon and Sydney.

However, by 6 May 1990 the *Sunday Times*, under the headline 'Holiday weather cools off', announced:

It's almost over. The heatwave that brought suntans, smiles and even red-rumped swallows from the Mediterranean will end tomorrow. After the hottest start to May since records began in 1875, cooler air will today stream from the north.

However, July and August saw the return of the amazing temperatures, but in the shorter heatwave the drought was less serious, although we again saw the pictures of dried and cracked farmland, and reservoirs once more exposing forgotten villages.

Among the very high temperatures recorded were 33.7°C (92.7°F) in Manchester, the highest August temperature since 1871, and 37.1°C (98.8°F) in Cheltenham, the latter exceeding the 1911 record of 36.7°C (98.1°F). Some of the disastrous effects of this exceptionally hot period were: many drownings; heathland fires; hosepipe bans; more deaths among old people due to heart attacks and strokes; subsidence of property; and fumes from cars, factories and power-stations producing lethal heat-smog. There was also an explosion of toxic blue-green algae in lakes and reservoirs, and in some areas pest control officers were called upon to deal with near-plagues of mice, ants and wasps.

Although the temperature of 37.1°C (98.8°F) at Cheltenham on 3 August is taken as a new record, we have an account of three weeks in June 1846 when the average temperature was 40.5°C (105°F), though this figure does not seem to have been confirmed and accepted. This heatwave and drought of 1846, although short, was apparently devastating, with many dying of heatstroke, fevers and drownings, and the streets of cities, particularly London, stinking with foul drains.

Droughts in the British Isles have been surprisingly common over the centuries, since the earliest recorded one in 298. In 678, *Agricultural Records* states 'Around this time there was a three year drought in southern England.' It was of this that the Venerable Bede wrote, 'The drought was such that a grievous famine fell upon the people, and piteously destroyed them.' Such droughts may occur perhaps only half a dozen times in a thousand years. It may be one of these that occurred in 1114, when the Thames was almost without water, and in October of that year was so dry that people could wade across.

With careful planning, controls, the use of water grids etc. possibly the worst effects of drought may be avoided, but only, it seems, at the cost of some personal discomfort and sacrifices made by people as a whole.

10 A Meteorological Miscellany

Storm Struck Steeple Ashton

At the west end of the church of St Mary the Virgin in the village of Steeple Ashton in Wiltshire is a brass tablet which describes a tragic event in the church's history:

> Upon this Tower was a Famous and Lofty Steeple, Containing in Height above the Tower 93 Foot; which a violent Storm of Thunder and Lightning rent a great Breach therein, July ye 25th in the year of our Lord 1670. The Parish willing to preserve such a Noble and Compleat Spyre, endeavoured to Repair the same by employing able workmen for that purpose. But such was the uncontrollable providence of Almighty God, that when it was almost finished, and the workmen Labouring thereon; another terrible Storm of Thunder and Lightning happened October 15th the same year, which threw down the Steeple ...

Two men, John Bartlett and John Robins, who were working on the steeple when the storm struck, were killed, and great damage was caused to the rest of the church. The repairs cost the parish the sum of £420 and were not completed for a further five years. The impressive steeple, which had stood for 250 years, was never rebuilt. The villagers may have wondered what they had done to deserve being singled out twice as the target of divine wrath, and would surely have thought it inconceivable that lightning should again strike Steeple Ashton.

However, just over a hundred years later, another violent electrical storm descended upon the village. It was described in a paper read to the Royal Society on 18 March 1773 entitled *Account of the Effects of Lightning at Steeple Ashton and Holt, in the county of Wilts on the 20th June, 1772, contained in several letters, communicated by Edward King, Esq., F.R.S.* One letter came from the Reverend Mr Eliot, whose vicarage in Steeple Ashton was struck during the storm. Mr Eliot was away from home at the time, but two other clergymen were staying there, and they gave detailed descriptions of their frightening experience. In the storm which began about midday the north chimney of the vicarage was struck by lightning. Mr Eliot wrote:

In the north parlour, to which this chimney belonged, were the Reverend Mr Wainhouse, of Steeple Ashton, and the Reverend Mr Pitcairn of Trowbridge, the former standing and the latter sitting in a great chair, with his back to the fire-place, near the wire of a bell ... As they were conversing about a loud clap of thunder that had just happened, they saw of a sudden a ball of fire between them, upon a level with the face of the former, and about a foot from it. They describe it to have been the size of a sixpenny loaf, and surrounded with a dark smoke; that it burst with an exceeding loud noise, like the firing of many cannons at once; that the room was instantly filled with the thickest smoke; and that they perceived a most disagreeable smell, resembling that of sulphur, vitriol, and other minerals in fusion; insomuch that Mr Pitcairn thought himself in danger of suffocation. Mr Wainhouse providentially received no hurt, except a slight scratch in his face from the broken glass that was flying about the room, a kind of stupefaction for some time, and a continued noise in his ears, which noise, the effect of the explosion, happened likewise to Mr Pitcairn and others in the house.

The lightning fell on Mr Pitcairn's right shoulder, made a hole in his coat, about a quarter of an inch in diameter, went under his arm in one line to his breast, descended from thence down the lower parts of his body in two irregular lines, about half an inch broad, attracted probably by his watch, the glass of which it shivered into small pieces, and meeting perhaps with a little resistance from it, spread itself around his body, and produced the sensation of a cord, tied close about his waist. A violent pain in his loins immediately followed; and from thence to his extremities there seemed to be a total stoppage of circulation, all sensation being lost, and his legs and feet resembling in colour and appearance those of a person actually dead. Besides shivering the glass of his watch, the lightning melted a little of the silver of it, and a small part also of half a crown in his pocket ... From the middle of his thigh the lightning went down the under side of it to the calf of his leg, and so to his shoe, which was *split into several pieces* in so remarkable a manner, as justly to claim the inspection of the curious. As soon as Mr Pitcairn was struck, he sank in his chair, but was not stunned; his face was blackened, and the features of it distorted. His body was burned in several places ... and he lost in some measure the use of his legs for two or three days; but by proper care he soon recovered, except a weakness and numbness in his right leg, which still remains.

The Reverend Mr Pitcairn, no doubt, felt lucky to be alive. Others who have survived lightning strokes have had their clothes and shoes torn to pieces or their watches and coins melted. The Reverend gentlemen seemed to have encountered ball lightning, the existence of which was denied for many years, and which is discussed in more detail on pages 173 and 175.

Two centuries later lightning struck Steeple Ashton again, the Bath and Wiltshire *Evening Chronicle* for Tuesday 26 June 1973, reporting that the aptly named Mr Henry Bolt, eighty-four years old, had been thrown across the kitchen of his cottage in High Street by the blast from a thunderbolt which struck a nearby barn. The gable end of the barn was smashed down, the roof set on fire, and £500 worth of hay destroyed. Mr Bolt lay dazed on his kitchen floor while farm workers struggled to extinguish the blaze at the barn. Mr Richard Matthews, who ran Bartletts Farm with his brother William, commented:

> It was a miracle that no one was killed. A minute later and we would have been in the barn unloading hay. I heard a bang, saw a blinding flash and smelled sulphur. The roof burst into flames and as I ran towards it I saw some of our pet pigeons lying blown to pieces. It could have been us.

Migratory Bogs

One of the most bizarre results of prolonged periods of rain is the creation of moving bogs. The phenomenon occurs predominantly in Ireland and Scotland, where there are extensive peat deposits, but cases have also been recorded in marshy regions of northern England, such as Chat Moss in Lancashire. John Leland, writing in the time of Henry VIII, reported:

> Chat Moss brast up within a mile of Mosley Haul and destroied much ground with mosse thereabout, and destroied much freshwater fishche thereabout, first corrupting with stinkinge water and mosse into Mersey Water, and Mersey corrupted carried the roulling mosse, part to the shores of Wales, part to the Isle of Man, and some unto Ireland.

Robert Chambers, compiler of the famous *Book of Days* published 1862/4, gave, in his *Domestic Annals of Scotland*, an account of a moving bog in Scotland in 1629:

> In the fertile district between Falkirk and Stirling, there was a large moss with a little lake in the middle of it, occupying a piece of gently rising ground. A highly cultivated district of wheat-land lay below. There had been a series of heavy rains, and the moss became

overcharged with moisture. After some days, during which slight movements were visible in the quagmire, the whole mass began one night to leave its native situation, and slid gently down to the low grounds. The people who lived on these lands, receiving sufficient warning, fled and saved their lives; but in the morning light they beheld their little farms, sixteen in number, covered six feet deep with liquid moss, and hopelessly lost.

A peat bog burst its bounds in 1697 at Charleville near Limerick in the Republic of Ireland, following a long period of rain. For some time a rumbling noise, resembling distant thunder, had been heard, coming from beneath the ground, and this was followed by the partially dried crust of the bog beginning to move, its convex upper surface sinking, and liquid mud flowing out at the edges. Chambers' *Book of Days* records:

> Not only did the substance of bog move, but it carried with it the adjacent pasture-grounds, though separated by a large and deep ditch. The motion continued for a considerable time, and the surface rose into undulations, but without bursting up or breaking. The pasture-land rose very high, and was urged on by the same motion, till it rested upon a neighbouring meadow, the whole surface of which it covered to a depth of sixteen feet.

The site which the bog had once occupied was left an unsightly scar, with holes containing foul-smelling water. Another moving bog was reported in 1727 near Draleen, some three miles from Charleville, in a broadsheet entitled *The Wonder of Ireland, Or, a strange and Surprising Account of the Moving Bog, near Draleen in the County of Limerick*. The bog, known as the Red Bog or The Common covered an area of some three hundred acres. The broadsheet reported that one part of the migratory bog covered 100 acres of farmland, mainly potato and corn fields, and a large meadow, in which only the tops of the trees protruded over the muddy slide. The broadsheet continues:

> Another part moved towards the Shannon; crossed a Road in the Barony of Cunloe, and Corkamahide, so as to make it unpassable, and the Water even black from the Shannon, by the Mold and Earth thereof; and hath continued this Motion either slower or quicker, according to the Declivity or Ascent it met with, for near 8 Days, whether now at its full period is not yet known.
> In its Motion broke large Trees, and turn'd up double Quickset-Hedges which stood in its way, and left in its room a vast Chasm of Water, and the like Bog and Mire. Its Motion may be computed, where the way was clear, and even, to be at the rate of

upwards of 2 Milles an Hour, and from its first Fixation, to the utmost extent, where it now is, near 2 English Miles.

Undoubtedly the most spectacular case of this type was that of Solway Moss which began to move after the heavy rain which deluged northern England and southern Scotland, and caused widespread and devastating floods in the autumn of 1771. Solway Moss, an expanse of bog about a mile to the north-west of Longtown in Cumberland, covered the top of a raised area of land, and was between two and three miles long, about a mile in breadth and covering about 1,600 acres. It consisted of a hard outer crust covering a vast muddy interior which was kept fluid by the water from several springs. At the base of the hill was a plain of fertile farm land, dotted with many small hamlets, each consisting of a farm and several houses. The whole area, Moss and farms, was owned by a Mr Graham of Netherby.

Even in the driest summer the Moss could be a dangerous place, one eighteenth-century writer stating that it was 'hardly safe for anything heavier than a sportsman and his gun.' In the time of Henry VIII, a large number of soldiers in the Scottish army, under the command of Oliver Sinclair, perished in the Moss, and many years later the skeleton of one of the men, still in armour, was found in the bog, along with the bones of his horse, by some peat-diggers. In normal weather the outer crust was strong enough to contain the semi-liquid interior, but in November 1771, the springs beneath the Moss were augmented by the exceptionally heavy rain, and at about midnight on Saturday the 17th, at a point on the easternmost side of the bog's crust which had been weakened by peat-diggers, the vast ocean of mud broke through.

The tide of thick black mud, studded with large lumps of peat, swept down the hill towards the plain, the noise alerting a farmer at the bottom of the hill. He searched for a lantern, and, looking out, saw what he first thought was his farmyard dung-heap mysteriously set in motion. Then the truth of the matter suddenly struck him and he rushed to warn his neighbours. According to the historian and naturalist Thomas Pennant (1723–98):

> Others received no other advice than what this Stygian tide gave them: some by its noise, many by its entrance into their houses; and I have been assured that some were surprised with it even in their beds. These passed a horrible night, remaining totally ignorant of their fate, and the cause of their calamity, till the morning, when their neighbours with difficulty got them out through the roof.

The disaster turned the ordered landscape of the plain, with its farms and enclosures, into a wasteland. Fields were covered by a vast carpet of mud, hedges eight or nine feet high being completely covered. Some houses disappeared completely beneath the black tide, a few actually being smashed down, while of others only the thatched roofs were visible. The road between Annan and Longtown was impassable for eight days.

News of the incident spread rapidly and people flocked from miles around to view the devastation. By the time the mud had stopped flowing, several weeks later, it was said to cover 1,000 acres of land and to be twenty feet deep in places. Four farms were only partially covered and still habitable, but twelve were completely destroyed, twenty-three families having to be evacuated. However, according to the *Newcastle Chronicle* of 14 December, 'Mr Graham has shown great humanity in giving the poor sufferers, who are all his tenants, every aid in his power', and an appeal was put out to raise money for those who had lost their homes and livelihoods.

In August 1861, heavy rains caused the movement of another Scottish bog. A farmer who lived near Aughingray Moss, between Slamannan and Airdrie, looked out one morning and saw, to his amazement, about twenty acres of the Moss detach itself from its clay bottom and slide along for a distance of about three-quarters of a mile. It was, the farmer said, a wonderful sight, but a large area of farmland was covered by the slide.

There have been several bog slides in and around Upper Teesdale in the north-east of England, W. Camden in *Britannica*, published in 1722, recording:

> ...about midsummer there happened an Eruption of Water of the Mosses; and the earth which was broken thereby is computed to be about 150 yards long and in some places 3 and in others 3 score yards broad and about 6 or 7 feet deep. Which great quantity of Earth being most of it carried by the flood of water into a neighbouring brook, and so into the River Bauder did great damage by overflowing the Meadows, and leaving behind it vast quantities of Mud ... It poisoned all the fish, not only in the foresaid Brook and the Bauder but also in the Tees for many miles.

Moving bogs have occurred more recently in the same area, following prolonged periods of rain, there being reports in 1870, near Meldon; in 1930, on Stainmore, and in 1963 on Meldon Hill. On the last occasion two slides occurred on the north-east slopes of the hill during a thunderstorm on the evening of 6 July 1963, the weather having been very wet over the previous few months. The slides left two scars in the blanket peat, about 250 yards long and 40 yards across at their widest points. It was estimated that some 207,000 cubic feet of material had been removed from the slopes.

There seem to be three main types of peat or bog slide, all caused by heavy rain. The first is the large-scale bog burst with a mass of almost liquid mud flowing out from beneath a hard crust; then there is the bog slide, which consists of the mass movement of peat or bog material for a considerable distance down from a slope but without the conversion of the material to liquid form, and finally the bog flow where, following tearing at the surface, there is a gradual movement down a slope for a few feet. The recent Meldon Hill movements would seem to be of the bog slide type.

Moving bogs are not so common as they were, due to the extensive draining of many peat lands, which mitigates the effects of heavy rain. The most recent case of a moving bog seems to be that in County Mayo, Ireland, where a 600-yard stretch of the coast road between Ballycastle and the village of Belderg was buried between 11.30 p.m. and 1.30 a.m. one night in December 1986. The migratory bog moved towards the sea, carrying with it a small plantation of trees and covering the road, which was eighteen feet wide, to a depth of four feet. The slide was discovered by a motorist who had to make a ten-mile detour to get home. The county had experienced an exceptionally wet summer and autumn, even by Irish standards. Interestingly, there is an Irish reel named the Moving Bog which can be found in Breandan Breathnach's *Ceol Rince Na Eireann (Dance Music of Ireland)*, published in 1963.

Thunderstones

In a house in Buntingford, Hertfordshire, which the author's mother visited when a child, were two stones, brown in colour, which stood on the tops of empty candlesticks on the mantelpiece. These stones, she was told, had hurtled to the pavement in the High Street during a thunderstorm. There was nothing especially interesting about them, they could have been turned up in a garden, but they were very heavy in relation to their size, and, when picked up during the storm they were hot.

For centuries it was widely believed that lightning and thunder were accompanied by missiles from the heavens – thunderbolts or thunderstones – and although scientists have always been sceptical of such beliefs there have been some detailed accounts of them,

The Times for 16 September 1852, for example, printed a letter from George E. Bayley, a chemist from Andover, Hampshire, who wrote:

> I have just examined a meteoric stone which, during a heavy thunderstorm last week, fell in the garden of Mr Robert Dowling, Lower Clatford, Andover. It is a 'martial pyrites' of an irregular surface, reddish-yellow in colour, without lustre, greyish yellow metallic fracture, about the size of a cricket ball, and weighing four pounds. It fell within six yards of the roof of the dwelling, and was picked up in the garden path immediately after the storm by his lady who had been watching the lightning ... I shall be pleased to favour any person with an inspection of the meteorolite who may call on me.

On 29 April 1868, during a violent thunderstorm over Birmingham, immense quantities of small stones were reported to have fallen in various parts of the city. They varied from about one-eighth of an inch to three-eighths of an inch in length and were about half these dimensions in thickness. The stones resembled small chips of Rowley Ragstone, a local geological formation, and it has been suggested that the stones had somehow been levitated by a whirlwind.

The Times for 26 April 1876, reported the finding of a 'meteorolite' near Wolverhampton:

> It is stated that about ten minutes to four, with a seven miles radius of the Wrekin, the villages were alarmed by an unusual rumbling noise in the atmosphere, followed immediately by an explosion resembling the discharge of heavy artillery ...
>
> About an hour after the report, a Mr George Brooks went into a meadow, which is in the occupation of his stepfather, Mr Bailey, and noticed that a hole had been cut in the ground. He probed it and found that what was apparently a hard stone had buried itself in the ground to a depth of 18 inches, passing through four inches of soil and fourteen inches of clay. It rested upon the gravel underneath these. The stone was dug up and removed to Wolverhampton where it was found to be a mass of meteoric iron ...

On 26 June 1880, a thunderstorm was passing over the Chelsea area of London, and at about 3.00 p.m. following an exceptionally loud clap of thunder, what appeared to be a ball of fire fell on the chimney stack of no. 180, Oakley Street. The servants, sitting in the kitchen, were suddenly alarmed by the room being filled with smoke and a heavy black mass coming down the chimney into the grate, where it shattered and threw fragments over the room. When the smoke had dispersed, among the debris in the grate was discovered a ball of about eight or nine inches in diameter 'like a cinder, with here and there fragments of metal in it.'

On 13 July 1909, at Ongar in Essex a meteoric stone was reported to have fallen into a stable yard during a thunderstorm, embedding itself eight inches in the gravel. The witness commented: 'The main part and fragments which we could collect weighed one pound thirteen ounces. The fall was witnessed by my daughters who were sheltering about eight yards away.'

C. Carus-Wilson gave a detailed report in an article in the journal *Knowledge* in 1885:

> I have frequently been struck by the fact of thunderbolts falling during violent storms, and of their simultaneous appearance with flashes of lightning. That masses of matter occasionally accompany the electric fluid when it reaches the earth there is no question; they have been seen and described as 'balls of fire', and I have in my possession one that fell some time ago at Casterton, in Westmoreland. It was seen to fall during a violent thunderstorm, and, killing a sheep *en route*, buried itself about six feet below the surface, and when dug out shortly after, it was still hot. In appearance it much resembles a volcanic bomb; it is about the size of a large coconut, weighs over 12 lbs, and seems to be composed of a hard ferruginous quartzite ... There is an external shell of about an inch in thickness, and this contains a nucleus of the same shape and material as the shell, but is quite independent of it, so that the one is easily separated from the other; I attribute this separation of the parts to an unequal cooling of the mass.

Three theories have been put forward to explain such reports: 1. That meteorites just happened to fall during thunderstorms; 2. That the stones did not actually fall during the storms and had been in the ground all along; 3. That the stones were lifted up and dropped by strong winds or tornadoes. A fourth and perhaps more likely explanation is that the lightning stroke, which may be carrying a current of thousands of amperes, produces great instantaneous heat which fuses ground material. However, all four explanations seem inadequate to account wholly for the phenomenon.

Devil's Work at Widecombe
In 1638 an unusually violent thunderstorm struck the church of St Pancras at Widecombe in the Moor, South Devon, a village famous for its association with Uncle Tom Cobbleigh and its

annual September fair on the green. We owe most of our knowledge of the storm to a contemporary pamphlet entitled *A True Relation of Those Sad and Lamentable Accidents which happened in and about the Parish Church of Withycombe in the Dartmoores, in Devonshire, on Sunday the 21 of October last, 1638*. This was printed in London on 17 November, just four weeks after the event, the tract selling so quickly that there was a reprint two days later. There seems to have been a third printing, of which the exact date is uncertain, and then a fourth on 27 November, by which time the authors, Thomas Wykes and Rothwell Warden, had gathered additional information from the witnesses. There were various other reprints over the years, some with verses and illustrations, the most recent being in 1905 under the title *The Widecombe Tracts, 1638, giving a contemporary Account of the Great Storm, reprinted with an introduction by J. Brooking Rowe*. This edition contains the tracts of 19 and 27 November 1638.

Wykes and Warden, reflecting a common belief of the time, assert that the storm was judgement from Heaven on a sinful world, but they seem to have been at pains to record accurately the historical details. The storm struck the church when some three hundred people were gathered there, the tracts recording that there fell:

> ...in time of Divine Service a strange darknesse, increasing more and more, so that the people there assembled could not see to reade any booke, and suddenly in a fearefull and lamentable manner, a mighty thundering was heard, the ratling whereof did answer much like unto the sound and report of many great Cannons, and terrible strange lightening therewith, greatly amazing those that heard and saw it, the darknesse increasing yet more, till they could not see one another; the extraordinarie lightening came into the Church so flaming, that the whole Church was presently filled with fire and smoke, the smell whereof was very loathsome, much like unto the sent of brimstone, some said they saw at first a great fiery ball come in at the window and passe thorough the Church, which so affrighted the whole Congregation that the most part of them fell downe into their seates, and some upon their knees, some on their faces, and some one upon another, with a great cry of burning and scalding, they all giving themselves up for dead, supposing the last Judgement day was come, and they had beene in the very flames of Hell ...

Several people were killed and many others seriously injured, Wykes and Warden sparing us none of the gruesome details. They record of one poor man that the lightning:

...strook off all the hinder part of the Warriner's head, the brains fell backward intire and whole into the next seats behind him, and two peeces of his scull, and dasht his blood against the wall, the other peece of his scull fell into the seate where he sate, and some of the skin of his head, flesh and haire was carried into the Chancell, and some of his haire to the quantity of a handfull, stuck fast as with lime and sand newley tempered upon one of the barres of the timberwork partission betweene the Church and the Chancell.

Many people were horribly burnt, including the wife of the minister, George Lyde, and one Mistress Ditford who was sitting next to her in the pew. One woman had her clothes set on fire as she attempted to run out of the church, and another 'had her flesh so torne and her body so grievously burnt, that she died the same night.' Another member of the congregation, Mr Hill, had his head battered against the church wall and also died that night. The tracts continue:

Some other persons were then blasted and burnt, and so grievously scalded and wounded, that since that time they have died thereof, and many other not like to recover, notwithstanding all the meanes that can bee procured to helpe them ... Also the Church it selfe was much torne and defaced by the thunder and lightening; and thereby also a beame was burst in the midst, and fell downe betweene the Minister and Clarke and hurst neither; and a weighty great stone, neare the Foundation of the Church is torne out and removed, and the steeple it selfe is much rent, and there where the Church was most rent, there was least hurt done to the people, and not any one was hurt either with the wood or stone, but a maid of Manaton, which came thither that afternoone to see some friends, whom Master Frynd the Coroner by circumstances, supposed she was kild with a stone. There were also stones throwne from the Tower and carried about a great distance from the Church, as thick as if a hundred men had beene there throwing, and a number of them of such weight and bignesse, that the strongest man cannot lift them. Also one Pinnacle of the Tower was torne downe and broke through into the Church.

Eventually the tempest abated, silence falling on the church, and one Ralph Rouse, a vintner, stood up and said 'Neighbours in the name of God shall we venture out of the Church?' The minister said that it was better to die in the church than elsewhere. Luckily, though, the storm had passed and the shaken congregation went out from the smoke-filled church into the daylight. The tracts conclude with the litany:

From lightening and tempest, from Plague
Pestilence and Famine, from Battell and murder, and from
suddaine death,
Good Lord deliver us.

At least five people died in the storm or later that day, and it is thought that several of the other fifty or sixty who were injured died later in the week. One of the victims, Roger Hill, is buried in the church where the centre lines of the nave and transepts cross, and his widow, who survived him by ten years, lies buried beside him.

It is generally accepted by meteorologists that the church was not merely struck by a thunderstorm, but by a tornado as well, there being several details in the tracts which suggest this, the tearing of huge stones from the church, for example. The tracts also record that several members of the congregation were lifted up and set down again unharmed; that a dog was whirled up into the air three times and then thrown down again dead, and that enormous hailstones fell during the storm, all features reminiscent of tornadoes. A 'fiery ball' is also described, and ball-lightning has been associated with tornadoes (see page 148). Finally, one early edition of the tracts was accompanied by a woodcut depicting what appears to be a funnel cloud emerging from the sky.

The storm soon became part of folklore, it being popularly believed that Satan himself had visited the church that day, one version of the story being that the Devil had come to snatch away the soul of Jan Reynolds while he was sleeping in church. 'Widecombe Jan', as he was known, was a notorious gambler, and it was rumoured that he had sold his soul to the Devil in exchange for skill at cards. Shortly before the storm struck, it was said that a mysterious stranger, clad all in black and riding a black horse, had stopped at the Tavistock Inn at Poundsgate and asked the way to Widecombe. He bought a pint of ale and the landlord was astonished when the ale hissed as it went down the stranger's throat, as if being poured on to flames. The man in black paid for his beer and galloped away, but the coins turned to dried leaves in the landlord's hand. Undoubtedly, the stranger was none other than the Devil himself, and during the storm he bore Widecombe Jan away on the back of his horse. The gambler's pack of cards spilled from his pocket and ever after it was said that if you looked across from the Warren Inn, you would see four small fields, each shaped like one of the four aces that fell over Vitifer and Birch

Tor. An account of the story in verse was written by Richard Hill, a schoolmaster, and this can be seen, mounted on two boards, inside the church, the plaque bearing at the bottom the names of two churchwardens, Peter and Sylvester Mann.

According to the Reverend E.C. Wood, in his guide to St Pancras's church, published in 1962, a child in a Devon school was once asked, 'What do you know of your ghostly enemy?', i.e. the Devil.

The boy replied, 'If you please ma'am, he lives at Widecombe.'

Showers of Animals

On the afternoon of 12 June 1954, Mrs Sylvia Mowdray took her young son and daughter to a display given by the Royal Navy in a park at Sutton Coldfield. After the exhibition they crossed the park to visit the fair, but were caught out in the open by a sudden heavy rain shower. Mrs Mowdray said:

> We tried to reach a belt of trees; and my four-year-old daughter put up her little umbrella and we heard these things thudding against it. When we looked, to our amazement, it was a shower of frogs. They were coming from the skies, hundreds of them. The umbrella was covered, all our shoulders were covered, and as we looked up we could see the frogs coming down like snowflakes.

An area of about fifty square yards was covered with the frogs which were between half and three-quarters of an inch long, and khaki-coloured with yellow flecks.

Rains of animals have been reported for centuries, perhaps the earliest account being that given by Pliny in his *Natural History* (AD 77) concerning a shower of fishes. One of the first British accounts was that given in a letter from Dr Robert Conny to Dr Robert Plot, author of *Natural History of Staffordshire* (1686):

> On Wednesday before Easter, Anno 1666, a Pasture Field at Cranstead near Wrotham in Kent, about two acres, which is far from any part of the Sea or Branch of it, and a Place where are no Fish Ponds, but a scarcity of Water, was all overspread with little Fishes, conceived to be rained down, there having been at that time a great Tempest of Thunder and Rain; the Fishes were about the Length of a Man's little Finger, and judged by all that saw them to be young whitings, many of them were taken up and showed to several Persons ... the Truth of it was averr'd by many that saw the Fishes lye scattered all over that Field, and none in the other Fields thereto adjoining; The Quantity of them was estimated to be about a Bushel, being all together.

Probably the most famous British fish fall was that which occurred at the village of Mountain Ash, four miles from Aberdare in Glamorganshire in February, 1859. One of the witnesses was John Lewis, a sawyer who worked for John Nixon, a prominent figure in the Welsh steam-coal trade. Lewis was interviewed shortly after the event by the Revd John Griffith, the vicar of Aberdare, at Nixon's yard, and stated:

> On Wednesday, 9th February, I was getting out a piece of timber for the purpose of setting it for the saw, when I was startled by something falling all over me – down my neck, on my head and on my back. On putting my hand down my neck I was surprised to find they were little fish. By this time I saw the whole ground covered with them. I took off my hat, the brim of which was full of them. They were jumping all about. They covered the ground in a long strip of about 80 yards by 12, as we measured afterwards. That shed [pointing to a very large workshop] was covered with them, and the chutes were quite full of them. My mates and I might have gathered bucketsful of them, scraping with our hands. We did gather a great many, about a bucketful, and threw them into the rain pool, where some of them now are. There were two showers, with an interval of ten minutes, and each shower lasted about two minutes or thereabouts.

Lewis added that it was about 11 a.m. when the incident occurred, the morning up-train to Aberdare was just passing, and it was a very wet morning, with a fairly strong wind blowing from the south-west. The fish seem to have fallen over quite a wide area of the Aberdare Valley (the *Cardiff and Merthyr Guardian* said they numbered several thousand), and many people, instantly aware that something very extraordinary had happened, quickly scooped up some of the fish and kept them alive for a while in fresh water. The fish were minnows and sticklebacks and several were sent to the Zoological Gardens at Regent's Park. In London the zoologists were sceptical, Dr. J.E. Gray of the British Museum asserting that someone had hoaxed John Lewis by throwing a bucket of water and fish over him, but all those who had investigated the case at first hand, such as the Reverend John Griffith, were quite convinced that the fish had indeed fallen just as Lewis described.

Another remarkable case was that concerning a shower of winkles which fell during an exceptionally severe thunderstorm which passed over Worcester at about three o'clock on the afternoon of Saturday 28 May 1881. The shower was preceded by a heavy fall of hail which stripped the leaves off trees and bushes and battered down crops. The *Worcester Daily Times* (30 May) reported:

> During the course of the storm a man named John Greenall, taking shelter in a shed in his master's garden at Comer-lane observed large masses of periwinkles fall, some of them being buried a considerable depth in the ground and others rebounding from the surface. The fall was confined to Comer-lane and the market garden belonging to Mr Leeds. Intelligence of what had happened soon got abroad, and an army of Worcester arabs took possession, and were as busy as diamond-diggers 'prospecting'. They gathered the periwinkles, which were in such profusion that one man alone succeeded in collecting two pecks. The search was prosecuted during the remainder of the day, and when darkness came on it was continued by the aid of lanterns. All day yesterday it was persevered in, and today the periwinkles are still being found. A live specimen is before us as we write. In one large shell, which a boy picked up in the lane and gave to Mr Joseph Phillips, of St John's, was a living hermit crab.

Charles Fort (1874–1932) famous for his pioneering writings on strange phenomena described many cases of animal showers, one of which concerned a rain of frogs, in 1921, at Southgate, now a suburb of north London but at that time out in the countryside. (See *The Complete Books of Charles Fort*.)

Remarkably, over fifty years later, writer Colin Bord traced one of the witnesses, Mrs J.M. Battell, who was six years old at the time and living with her parents and sister at Tottenham. In 1977, she described to Colin Bord how they were all enjoying a day's outing to Southgate on 17 August:

> We were walking along a country road, with hedges on either side and a ditch on the left. It began to rain very heavily and we took shelter under a tree standing beside a farm gate up a little farm track on the left of the road. When the shower stopped we emerged to find the road literally swarming with tiny frogs. The size of the body was about half an inch long with four little legs in proportion to the body size.

The family stood and stared as the tiny creatures slowly made their way to the sides of the road and disappeared in the hedges and the ditch, till not a frog was to be seen and no evidence of the occurrence remained. (See 'Falls' by R.J.M. Rickard, *Fortean Times*, no.24.)

Curiously, while there have been many accounts of young frogs falling in rain showers, reports of tadpoles and fully grown specimens are extremely rare. I have seen no accounts of rains of large frogs in Britain and have come across only one brief reference to tadpoles. This appeared in the *Maidenhead Advertiser* for 4 December 1981 where Leonard Burrough, eighty years old, was recalling his early years in Maidenhead. One afternoon, probably in 1910, young Leonard walked out into the High Street after a terrific thunderstorm and to his amazement found it, 'alive with thousands of tiny frogs and tadpoles.'

Occasionally the showers are not of living but of dead animals, such as occurred at Hendon, a suburb of Sunderland, on the afternoon of Saturday 24 August 1918. At about three o'clock a group of allotment-holders were sheltering in their sheds during a heavy thunderstorm when they saw small fish falling to the ground. Several hundred fish, later identified as sand eels, fell in nearby Commercial Road, Canon Cocker Street and Ashley Street, as well as on the adjacent allotments – an area of about a third of an acre. They were dead and stiff, some breaking as they hit the ground.

Showers of animals have continued to be reported up to the present day, there being accounts of frogs (Bedford, July 1979); crabs (Swansea, September 1981, and Brighton, June 1983); winkles and a starfish (Thirsk, Yorkshire, June 1984) and fish (East Ham, east London, May 1984).

The east London fish fall was investigated by Bob Rickard, editor of the *Fortean Times*. He interviewed the main witness, Ronald Langton, on 5 June 1984, when he was told that a builder, Edward Rodmell, arriving to work at Mr Langton's house on 28 May, had found two fish, resembling dabs, in the back yard, and another, more like a whiting, on a heap of rubble. It was a narrow yard, and as it seemed likely that they had fallen from above, the two men had looked out of an upstairs window from where they saw another fish, like a whiting, lying on the back roof of the house. When Bob Rickard arrived on 5 June, he was shown the two flat fish (the pile of rubble and the other fish had by then been cleared away). Mr Langton climbed a ladder to retrieve the fish still lying on the roof and found two more pieces of fish, a head and tail, which were in the guttering.

Thinking back, Mr Langton recalled that on the night of the 26/27 May there was a thunderstorm with one heavy downpour and several lighter showers. While watching the late television he had heard slapping sounds, and with hindsight thought that these might have been caused by the fish falling on to the roof. Mrs Langton also remembered that while walking along Green Street on the day the fish had been found in their yard, she had seen another one lying in the gutter, near Upton Park underground station. No fish had been found in any properties adjacent to Mr Langton's and he had seen none on other roofs while he was up the ladder.

Bob Rickard took the fish to the Natural History Museum where the flat fish were identified as flounders and the other as a smelt. At the museum it was suggested that a waterspout might have lifted the fish from the Thames, only a couple of miles away, or the Essex coast, but there had been no reports of waterspouts, and the London Weather Centre, when contacted, stated that the weather at the time of the fish fall had not been conducive to their formation.

The *Newham Recorder* printed the story on 7 June, giving Bob Rickard's telephone number, and that evening he was telephoned by a man who had found about thirty fish in his garden at Canning Town, about one-and-a-half miles east of Mr Langton's house. The caller promised to get in touch later with more details, but never did. There was another call from the Canning Town area, this time from a man saying that he had found four fish in his garden, but he too seemed reluctant to co-operate further. Bob Rickard concluded:

> I do not think the events were a practical joke. Their locations were too far apart, too obscure, and the buildings were too high to lob fish over; and no one came forward. On the contrary, the facts, such as they are, conform to the general pattern of such falls historically.

The foregoing are a few examples of animal showers which have been reported in Britain, but it is a world-wide phenomenon. Scientists no longer dispute that such falls occur, but how can they be explained? The standard explanation is that they are the result of waterspouts or tornadoes sucking up fish and other creatures from their normal habitats and later releasing them. This leaves some points still not satisfactorily answered:

1. Very occasionally waterspouts have been seen to suck up fish from the sea and then scatter them, but one would expect that there would be far more eyewitness accounts of such occurrences than are reported.
2. There is the curious selectivity of animal showers. Usually only one or two species of animals fall from the sky, and they are unaccompanied by mud, weed debris, or the wide range of small

animal life that one would expect to come from ponds, lakes or the sea. The absence of tadpole falls has already been mentioned.

3. Animal showers seem generally to be confined to a very small area, whereas tornadoes and waterspouts scatter their loads widely.

4. Animal showers often occupy a fairly long period of time, sometimes ceasing temporarily and then starting again. Occasionally, the animals are dead when they fall, which also suggests that they have been aloft for long periods.

These features are not fully explained by the tornado theory. If tornadoes are responsible for animal rains, the mechanics of the process are very far from being understood.

Showers of Seeds and Nuts

Even more bizarre, perhaps, than showers of animals are the rains of seeds, nuts and other vegetable matter which have also been reported since ancient times. A typical modern case was that reported by Alfred Wilson Osborne of Bristol, who on the morning of the 13 March 1977 was walking home from church with his wife. They were passing a car showroom when Mr Osborne heard a click on the pavement as if a button had fallen off his jacket. Looking down he saw a hazelnut and suddenly he and his wife were caught in a shower of nuts which bounced off the pavement and 'pinged' on the nearby cars: Mr Osborne estimated that between 350 and 400 nuts had fallen. About three minutes later a friend rushed up in great excitement – he too had been caught in the shower of nuts. The Osbornes were baffled by the shower – it seemed impossible that anybody could have been playing a trick on them, and the weather at the time was fine with a clear sky and no wind. The mystery was compounded by the fact that hazelnuts are not in season until the autumn, yet these nuts were ripe and fit to eat, as Mr Osborne discovered when he sampled one. 'It's impossible to account for it,' he commented, 'how they came and where they came from I have no idea. I have thought that it might be a vortex which sucked them up, but I don't know where you suck up hazelnuts in March!'

Even more strange were the showers of seeds and beans that were reported at Southampton two years later. At about 9.30 on the morning of 12 February 1979, Roland Moody, a keen gardener, was planting seedlings in the conservatory at the back of his house when he heard a whooshing sound on the glass above him. He didn't take a lot of notice of it and continued with his work but about three-quarters of an hour later it happened again. He looked up and found that the whole of the glass above him was covered in what was afterwards found to be mustard and cress seed. The falls were repeated some five or six times throughout the day, the whole of Mr Moody's garden being covered with mustard and cress seed, a curious detail being that the seeds were coated with a strange jelly-like substance.

He spoke to his next-door neighbour, Mrs Stockley, and found that the seeds had fallen on her property as well. Furthermore, Mrs Stockley said that about a year previously mustard and cress seed had fallen on her garden, but she had not spoken to anyone about it at the time. The following day there was a shower of peas, maize and haricot beans, this time the seeds also falling on the garden of Mr and Mrs Gale, the neighbours on the other side of Mr Moody. These falls were repeated over the next few days, and on one occasion a shower of beans was blown into the Gale's open front door, with such force that they travelled ten feet along the hall and into the kitchen. There were at least twenty-five falls of seed and beans and the Stockleys even called in the police to investigate the mystery, but nothing could be found to account for the showers. Eventually, the puzzled recipients of the seeds gave up trying to find an explanation, and decided to turn them over in their gardens: 'I cleared eight full buckets of mustard and cress from the garden', recalled Mr Moody, while the Gales and the Stockleys produced bumper crops of beans.

Curiously, the seeds fell on only three houses in the street, and to this day the occurrence remains a mystery, though there was a vague report that a boy in the street had seen the seed coming down in torrents from a small, very dark cloud in the sky.

A vegetable shower was experienced by Trevor Williams of Tonna, near Neath in South Wales. Working on his garden pool on an April day in 1980, he heard a 'plopping' sound which he first took to be raindrops, but he then realized that dried peas were falling all around him. 'I could not believe my eyes,' he said, 'there were peas everywhere. They were bouncing off the greenhouse and house roof in their thousands. The storm lasted several minutes and I was able to collect several jam-jars full of peas.'

The Meteorological Office regard such occurrences in a very matter of fact way. Roger Hunt, a spokesman at Bracknell, said that many such falls had been reported, adding, 'What happens is that strong vertical airlifts or mini-tornadoes take things into the sky and then winds take them sideways. They join cloud formations and come down mixed with rain.' As in the case of animal showers, however, this explanation seems hardly adequate to account for all aspects of the phenomenon.

The Ice Bomb Mystery

On Monday 2 April 1973, there had been mixed weather over the north of England: gales and heavy rain over the Yorkshire coast, gusts of 110 m.p.h. being recorded at Whitby; fog over the Mersey, causing shipping to be temporarily suspended; while in Manchester there had been a moderate fall of snow in the morning, giving way to clearer skies in the afternoon.

At exactly 7.54 p.m., Dr R.F. Griffiths (a postgraduate student at Manchester University) walking along Burton Road near Withington Hospital, was startled by a single flash of lightning – noticed by many people because of its intensity and the fact that there were no further flashes. Dr Griffiths was a lightning observer for the Electrical Research Organization and he carefully noted the time and nature of the strike and the prevailing conditions. (He later learned that hail had fallen in Wilmslow at the time of the lightning.) As he returned along Burton Road shortly after, at 8.03, a large object crashed on to the road to his left and about ten feet ahead, exactly at the junction of Burton Road and Bottesford Avenue. The missile was made of ice, numerous fragments of which were now widely scattered over the street. Dr Griffiths retrieved the largest piece and dashed home. He preserved the chunk of ice in the freezer compartment of his refrigerator, later transferring it, carefully insulated, to his laboratory at UMIST. The ice block was 5½ inches long and weighed 22 ounces, and probably formed about a third of the original block.

How had the ice bomb been formed? In some respects it was similar to a hailstone, having layers of clear ice (fifty-one in number) separated by thinner layers of trapped air bubbles. However, the complete ice bomb could have weighed as much as 4½ lbs, thus making it considerably larger than the famous giant hailstone from Coffeyville in Kansas, at 1½ lbs, the world's largest recorded hailstone. Furthermore, it differed from a normal hailstone in that its crystals were much larger, and its layers of ice much more regular. Could it have been formed artificially – a hoax? Dr Griffiths tried to create a similar block by filling balloons with water and hanging them in a refrigerator, but the resulting structures bore no resemblance to the ice bomb. In the balloons the water froze from the outside in, leaving an unfrozen pocket at the centre, and when this pocket eventually froze the resultant stress fractured the rest of the block.

Could the ice bomb have fallen from a plane? Dr Griffiths made enquiries at Manchester's Ringway Airport and found that two aircraft had passed over the area at the approximate time of the incident, one landing at 8.01 and the other at 8.06. There were, however, three reasons why he ruled out the hypothesis:

Firstly, if such a large growth of ice had built up on an aircraft it would have been on a fairly small component, such as a radio antenna. The aerodynamic forces on such a body during flight would be enormous, inevitably causing damage to the component, and specific enquiries showed that no damage had occurred to the two aircraft in question, or indeed to any others airborne at the time.

Secondly, he pointed out that:

The shape of an ice growth starting from a small nucleus on an aircraft at normal flight speed would be expected to exhibit far greater elongation in the airstream direction than is displayed by this body, where the degree of growth in the direction parallel and perpendicular to the major axis is the same within a factor of 2; such a mode of growth is consistent with all known characteristics of hailstones and it is hard to visualise how it could have occurred on an aircraft.

Thirdly, if such a thick growth of ice occurred at one part of an aircraft one would have expected heavy icing over other forward facing surfaces and, as already pointed out, no such icing had been reported on any other aircraft in the air at that time.

Dr Griffiths concludes:

The ice sample displays a puzzling collection of features. Whilst it is clearly composed of cloud water, there is no conclusive evidence enabling one to decide how it grew, except that laboratory tests suggest that this sample did not grow in a container. In some respects it is very much like a hailstone, whilst in others it is not. Equally, the possibility that it was formed by icing on an aircraft is not borne out by the flight records.

There have been reports of ice-block falls for centuries, though it is rare for a specimen to be examined so thoroughly as that investigated by Dr Griffiths. Some are less than twelve inches in diameter and weigh four or five pounds, while others may be three feet thick and weigh a hundred pounds. Some are of clear ice while others have a layered structure or consist of enormous aggregations of small hailstones. Some are spherical while others are irregular in shape. They may fall in fine weather, during thunderstorms, or sometimes, like the Manchester specimen, after a single flash of lightning. The explanation generally put forward today is that the ice bombs have probably fallen from an aircraft – possibly the discharge from an aircraft toilet, but this is not very satisfactory and in any case cannot account for the well-documented incidents which predate air travel.

Some notable cases are briefly described below:

1811: Chunks of ice a foot in diameter fell in Derbyshire on May 12th.

1849: On the evening of 13 August a mass of ice some twenty feet in circumference fell on an estate at Ord in Ross-shire. *The Times* of the following day stated that, 'It had a beautiful crystalline appearance, being nearly all quite transparent, if we except a small portion of it which consisted of hailstones of uncommon size fixed together. It was principally composed of small squares, diamond-shaped, of from one to three inches in size all firmly congealed together.'

1860: During a snowstorm on 16 March at Upper Wasdale, Cumbria, huge blocks of ice fell, resembling, when seen from a distance a flock of sheep.

1908: On 2 July, at Braemar, Grampian, on a clear day when the sun was shining, thunder was heard and large pieces of ice fell from the sky.

1950: On a November day, a farm near North Molton in Devon was showered with chunks of ice, 'the size of dinner plates.' Lying amongst the ice blocks was a dead sheep, its neck cleanly cut through by a jagged lump of ice weighing fourteen pounds.

1973: On 9 January an ice block weighing ten pounds fell from the sky, smashing a porch at West Wickham, Kent.

1974: On 25 March a cube-shaped block of ice, some eighteen inches square, crashed on to a car at Pinner in Middlesex. A spokesman for the Civil Aviation Authority said it had probably come from a plane, perhaps seepage from waste tanks, or snow mixed with oil which had been dislodged from a plane's undercarriage. He added that it would be almost impossible to establish which plane it had come from.

1980: On 14 April, a chunk of ice crashed through the roof of a house in Lyndhurst, Hampshire. The householder, after collecting the pieces of ice which were strewn over a bedroom floor, estimated that the ice bomb was the size of a large bucket.

1980: The *Western Morning News* (Devon edition) for 2 October, reported that Mrs Sandra Fox, of Plymouth and her two children narrowly escaped death when an ice bomb smashed through the roof of their home in Southway Drive. The block made a two-foot hole in the roof and bedroom ceiling and shattered into pieces about two feet from her and the young children. At about the same time, another block of ice crashed through the roof of a nearby bungalow, the householder, Mrs Pidgeon reporting that it was preceded by a terrifying whistle, like a shell flying.

It is possible that there may be several different sources of ice bombs. Some may be congealed masses of ordinary hailstones; some, as the authorities claim, may indeed fall from aircraft; some are almost certainly the result of meteorological processes not yet understood. It is even possible, as Arthur C. Clarke has suggested, that some ice meteors have an extra-terrestrial origin, being the debris from comets.

After fishes, frogs, nuts, seeds and ice blocks, one might wonder what else could fall from the skies. In fact, over the years an amazing variety of showers of bizarre objects has been reported, such as hay, wheat, ash, cinders, sand, fossil shells, berries, insects, clumps of earth and grass and gelatinous 'blobs'. These have been well documented and many of the cases are described in the works of Charles Fort, William R. Corliss and in the pages of *Fortean Times*.

This book has recounted stories of extreme weather, not from the scientific viewpoint but that of ordinary people in situations beyond their control. Today we have amazingly accurate weather forecasting, but can still be taken by surprise and able to do little but try to protect ourselves and our property. Like previous generations, we remain relatively helpless in the face of freak weather.

Bibliography

Andrews, William, *Famous Frosts and Frost Fairs in Great Britain, Chronicled from the Earliest to the Present Time* (Redway, London, 1887)

Barnes, F.A. & King, C.A.M., 'A Tornado at Tibshelf, Derbyshire', *Weather*, vol.7, no.7 (July 1952)

Bennett, Alfred Rosling, *Historic Locomotives and Moving Accidents by Steam and Rail* (Cassell, London, 1906)

Billett, H., 'The South Wales Tornado of October 27, 1913', *Geophysical Memoir*, no.11 (HMSO, London, 1914)

Blackmore, R.D., *Lorna Doone* (London, 1869)

Bonacina, L.C.W., 'The Widecombe Calamity of 1638' *Weather*, vol.1, pp.122–5 (1946)

Bowen, David, *Britain's Weather. Its Workings, Lore and Forecasting* (David & Charles, Newton Abbot, 1973)

Carr, Revd E. Donald, *A Night in the Snow* (First published 1865, Clark & Howard Books, Wolverhampton, 1984)

Chambers, R., *The Book of Days* (W. & R. Chambers, London, 1862/4)

Corliss, William R., *Tornadoes, Dark Days, Anomalous Precipitation and Related Weather Phenomena* (The Sourcebook Project, Glen Arm, USA)

Crisp, D.T., Rawes M. & Welch, D., 'A Pennine Peat Slide', the *Geographical Journal*, vol.130, part 4 (Dec. 1964)

Davis, G., *Frostiana* (G. Davis, London, 1814)

Defoe, Daniel, *The Storm or, A collection of the most remarkable casualties and disasters which happened in the late dreadful tempest, both by sea and land* (G. Sawbridge, London, 1704)

Fort, Charles, *Complete Books of Charles Fort* (Dover, New York, 1974)

Grieve, H., *The Great Tide* (Essex County Council, 1959)

Griffiths, R.F., 'Observation and Analysis of an Ice Hydrometeor of Extraordinary Size', *Meteorological Magazine*, vol. 104, no. 1238 (September 1975)

Harrison, Robert, *A Strange relation of the Suddain and Violent Tempest which happened at Oxford May 31, Anno Domini 1682* (Richard Sherlock, Oxford, 1682)

Hawke, E.L., 'Rainfall in a "Cloudburst".' *Nature* (2 Feb 1952)

Hill, George, *Hurricane Force* (Collins, London, 1988)

Hinkson, G.A., 'Well-defined Rain Area', *Meteorological Magazine* (Aug. 1932)

Holford, Ingrid, *British Weather Disasters* (David & Charles, Newton Abbot, 1976)

——, *The Guinness Book of Weather Facts and Feats* (Guinness Superlatives, London, 1977)

Hone, William, *The Everyday Book* (Hunt & Clarke, London, 1827)

Hood, J. Dennis, *Waterspouts on the Yorkshire Wolds. Cataclysm at Langtoft and Driffield* (B. Fawcett, Driffield, 1892)

Lamb, H.H., 'Tornadoes in England. May 21, 1950', *Geophysical Memoir*, no.99 (HMSO, London, 1957)

Lane, Frank, *The Elements Rage* (David & Charles, Newton Abbot, 1966)

——, *The Violent Earth* (Croom Helm, London, 1976)

Lauder, Sir Thomas Dick, *An Account of the Great Floods of August, 1829 in the Province of Moray and Adjoining Districts* (J. McGillivray & Son, Elgin, 1873)

Laughton, L.G. Carr & Heddon, V., *Great Storms* (P.Allan, London, 1930)

Lovell, John, 'Thunderstorm, Cloudburst and Flood at Langtoft, East Yorkshire, July 3rd, 1892', *Quarterly Journal of the Royal Meteorological Society* (Jan. 1893)

Marsden, Fiona, 'Lewes Avalanche', *Sussex Archaeological Society Newsletter*, no.47 (Dec. 1985)

Meaden, G.T., 'Point Deluge and Tornado at Oxford, May, 1682', *Weather*, no.34 (1979)

——, 'Four Storm Stories from Steeple Ashton', *Weather* (Dec. 1973)

——, 'The Earliest known British and Irish Tornadoes', *J. Met. UK*, vol. 1, no.3 (Dec. 1975)

—— 'A Meteorological Explanation for some of the Mysterious Sightings on Loch Ness and other Lakes and Rivers', *J. Met. UK*, vol. 1, no.4 (Jan. 1976)

—— 'The Fastnet Race Disaster', *J. Met. UK*, vol. 4, no.43 (Nov. 1979)

—— 'The Fastnet Race Inquiry', *J. Met. UK*, vol. 5, no.45 (Jan. 1980)

Michell, John & Rickard, R.J.M., *Living Wonders. Mysteries and Curiosities of the Animal World* (Thames & Hudson, London, 1982)

——, *Phenomena: a Book of Wonders* (Thames & Hudson, London, 1977)

Pollard, Michael, *North Sea Surge. The Story of the East Coast Floods of 1953* (Terence Dalton, Lavenham, 1978)

Rickard, R.J.M. 'Falls', *Fortean Times*, no.24 (Winter 1978)

—— 'Fishes Fall in East London', *Fortean Times*, no.42 (Autumn 1984)

——, 'Why did the Peat Bog Cross the Road?', *Fortean Times*, no.54 (Summer 1980)

Rowe, J. Brooking, *The Two Widecombe Tracts, 1638, giving a Contemporary Account of the Great Storm. Reprinted with an Introduction* (James G. Commin, Exeter, 1905)

Rowe, M.W., 'The earliest documented tornado in the British Isles, Rosdalla, County Westmeath, Eire, April, 1054', *J. Met. UK*, vol. 14, no.137 (Mar. 1989)

——, 'A History of Tornado Study in Britain', *J. Met. UK*, vol. 1, no.1 (Oct. 1975)

——, 'Tornadoes in Medieval Britain', *J. Met. UK*, vol. 1, no.7 (Apr. 1976)

Schadewald, Robert, 'The Great Fishfall of 1859', *Fortean Times*, no.30 (Autumn 1979)

Shellard, H.C., 'Collapse of Cooling Towers in a Gale, Ferrybridge, 1. November, 1965', *Weather*, vol. 22, no.6 (June 1967)

Stevens, L.P., 'Waterspouts in the English Channel', *Weather*, vol. 31, no.13 (Mar. 1976)

Stirling, Robin, *The Weather of Britain* (Faber & Faber, London, 1982)

Summers, Dorothy, *The East Coast Floods* (David & Charles, Newton Abbot, 1978)

Thomas, John, *The Tay Bridge Disaster. New Light on the 1879 Tragedy* (David & Charles, Newton Abbot, 1972)

Thomson, W., *To the Memory of those who suffered from the Lewes Avalanche in 1836* (*Sussex Express*, Lewes, 1863)

Unknown, *Narrative of the Dreadful Disasters occasioned by the Hurricane, which visited Liverpool and Various Parts of the Kingdom, on the Nights of Sunday and Monday, January 6th and 7th, 1839* (*Liverpool Mercury*, Liverpool, 1839)

Vonnegut, B. & Ryan, R.T., 'Miniature Whirlwinds Produced in the Laboratory by High Voltage Electrical Discharges, *Science*, vol.168, no.1349 (1970)

Welfare, Simon & Fairley, John, *Arthur C. Clarke's Mysterious World* (William Collins, London, 1980)

Wethered, E., 'A Waterspout', *Nature*, (20 June 1878)

Wright, John, 'When an avalanche destroyed a Christmas', *Sussex Life* (Dec. 1987)

Index

190